THE
FOUNDATION
—OF—
WEALTH

THE
FOUNDATION
OF
WEALTH

A BIBLICAL PERSPECTIVE ON HARVESTING WEALTH

ALISHA N. SCOTT

THE FOUNDATION of WEALTH

By Alisha N. Scott

Published by Alisha Scott Enterprises

www.alishascott.org

alisha@alishascott.org

Unless otherwise noted, all Scripture quotations are from the Amplified Bible, Old Testament Copyright© 1965, 1987 by Zondervan Cooperation. The Amplified New Testament Copyright© 1954, 1958, 1987 by Zondervan Cooperation. Used by permission.

Scripture quotations marked KJV are from the King James Version of the Bible.

Scripture quotations marked EXB are from the Expanded Version of the Bible. Copyright© 2011 by Thomas Nelson. Used by permission. All rights reserved.

Scripture quotations marked VOICE are from the Voice™. Copyright © 2012 by Ecclesia Bible Society. Used by permission. All rights reserved.

Scripture quotation marked NIV are from the Holy Bible, New International Version. Copyright© 1973, 1978, 1987 by the Lockman Foundation. Used by permission.

ISBN-978-0-578-46557-9

First Edition

14 13 12 11 10/ 10 9 8 7 6 5 4 3 2 1

Printed in the United States of America

DEDICATION

To my grandparents, Garfield, and Mattie Freeman thank you for providing a foundational base upon which to write this book. Thank you for being faithful tillers of the earth. To my parents, Roosevelt, and Bernice Scott thank for your unlimited support and love. To my sisters, nieces and nephews thank you for supplying me with support, laughter and smiles during the darkest times of my life. To Cathy Greene, thank you for always being there no matter what.

CONTENTS

INTRODUCTION

AS I REMINISCE OF days spent on my grandparent's farm, many quaint memories flood my heart. I can almost smell the earthy fragrance of the fresh soil upon which my grandfather planted seeds of almost any vegetable or fruit to be imagined. The aroma of fresh vegetables comes to mind as I recall "shelling" peas and "shucking" corn on my grandmother's front porch. I remember sitting at her table watching her turn raw ingredients into delicious soup right before my eyes. My taste buds ignite thinking of juicy, hand-picked peaches and sweet pear preserves grandmother made from scratch. I'd feasted on fresh produce of the land. I was fed, and I was full but oblivious to the demanding process of seedtime and harvest.

> *The farmer knows how to wait patiently for the land to produce vegetables and fruits. He cannot harvest a freshly planted seed. Instead, he waits for the early and the late showers to nourish the soil.*
>
> *James 5:7b, VOICE*

As a child, I didn't comprehend the vast amount of labor my grandfather endured as a farmer. My mind couldn't fathom or appreciate the process by which the crops arrived in my belly. Seedtime and harvest involved not only blossoming fruit and tasty preserves. You couldn't just walk up on a harvest. Crops didn't just mysteriously appear on grocery store shelves or on dinner plates without process. It was only as an adult that I learned to respect the beauty of my grandfather's strenuous effort as a tiller of the earth. From seed, he could produce a harvest and fill the bellies of his famished family. Farming took toil. Sowing required faith. Planting necessitated patience. Harvesting demanded process.

> As long as the earth endures, seedtime and harvest, cold and heat, summer and winter, day and night will never cease.
>
> Genesis 8:22

Harvesting after seedtime is an inevitable and never-ending cycle implemented by the Creator of the heavens and the earth. However, before God spoke of yielding a harvest, He first prepared the earth (see Genesis 1:9, 11-12). A harvest cannot be gathered without seed having first entered rich, tilled land. Tilling is another word for *plowing*. When land is plowed its soil is "cut, turned over, and pulverized." Plowing literally crushes and slices through the soil. However, during the cutting, the plow removes undesirable roots, such as weeds. This step is vital because weeds compete with crops for space, light, water, nutrients, and energy. Often poisonous, they will choke the life out of what's been planted if they're not dealt with. Tillage is necessary so that the land is matured and what's planted in the earth has fertile soil to thrive in.

Once the soil has been prepared, the seed can properly be introduced into the earth. When I think of sowing seed, it's difficult to fight images of a smiling farmer holding handfuls of seeds casually throwing them onto the ground. This short-sightedness couldn't be further from the truth. Sowing entails much more than sporadically distributing seed. In fact, it usually involves the use of a *harrow*. A harrow is an agricultural tool with spiked teeth drawn over freshly plowed land to level it and remove any remaining weeds. It is also used so that the seed travels deep into the earth without difficulty.

A necessary process of growth takes place between sowing and harvesting; this is when the plant grows its roots. During this stage, the farmer is aware that seed is in good ground because he planted it, not because it's visible. It would take months—depending on what's planted—for there to be any evidence to the natural eye that there's even something there. The seed is buried deep into the earth, looked over, stepped on and rained upon. Finally, when its roots are sturdy, the plant emerges and breaks through the soil. Breaking through is not as easy as it sounds because to [1]emerge is "to rise from an inferior or unfortunate state or condition." Physically, the plant is at a disadvantage in that it must have the fortitude to push through the formidable elements of the earth. Though difficult, it's unavoidable because in order for the plant to become visible and produce fruit, it must emerge. It is only after the plant arises fully grown that it can be harvested.

WEALTH • HARVESTER /welth-hahr-vuh-ster/ noun
A philanthropist who gathers wealth to gather a
harvest of souls for the kingdom of God.

---

[2]*Harvesting* is the process of gathering ripe crops from the field. Marking the end of a growth cycle, it is a method used to collect *mature* crops after the season of planting and developing. Simply speaking, harvesting is the time when a farmer literally reaps of the earth what has been sown into the earth. Likewise,

wealth harvesters gather the wealth of the earth to fill the bellies of God's children. They are special givers called to gather souls at the end time harvest by funding kingdom endeavors. While the call to harvesting wealth sounds exciting, it's no easy feat. Those called to tremendous wealth are often called to harrowing experiences. The word harrow also means " pain and distress to the mind and feelings." To harrow is to "devastate, ruin, strip and break down." Harvesters of wealth will experience various trials and circumstances—used by God—to root, ground, and develop them. It is in that place of development where you will be stepped on and overlooked but also must have faith knowing you have sown seed into good ground. The world can't see you because God has hidden you to mature you. And you cannot be introduced into the earth until you have been harrowed.

Wealth harvesters don't just appear, they emerge. There is breakthrough on the other side, but you have to break through resistance to get it. Harvesting wealth entails a groundbreaking growth process by which the *Husbandman* matures you by ruining and stripping you. God must till the soil of your heart. He will pulverize your flesh so that you bear good, developed fruit in due season.

GOD, THE HUSBANDMAN

> *I am the true vine, and my Father is the husbandman. Every branch in me that beareth not fruit he taketh away: and every branch that beareth fruit, he purgeth it, that it may bring forth more fruit.*
>
> *John 15:1-2, KJV*

The term *husbandman* is rarely used today but is simply another word for "farmer" or "worker of the soil." While earthly farmers till the soil of the earth, God—the

Introduction

Husbandman—tills the soil of our souls. It is while the Husbandman is tilling your soil, that He inspects every branch that is attached to Jesus, the Vine. If what He finds is unfruitful, He "purges" it. Much like plowing, to ³*purge* is to "rid whatever is impure or undesirable." An interesting synonym for *purge* is "shakeups." God, the Sovereign Tiller of our beings will shake up everything in our lives to shake loose the weeds holding us back from reaping good fruit.

⁴*Reaping* is the cutting of grain for harvest, typically using a scythe, sickle, or reaper. We get excited when "it's harvest time," and rightly so. Harvest time brings joy and a sense of finality to a season of arduous labor. However, most fail to realize that when it's "harvest time," it's simultaneously "reaping time" because along with the harvest of fruit comes the reaper that cuts it. The husbandman *must* cut it. If not, fully developed fruit will wither away and die in the very place it was planted and blossomed in.

In a dream, I sat on the floor with my waist cut from one side to the other. God said, "I will do whatever I have to do to get My word out." Realistically, a cut to that degree would have been fatal. However, in the dream, there was no blood or enduring pain; it was not unto death. It is a fact that over-tilling can cause more harm than it does good, but the Husbandman knows exactly where to cut us to grow us. And though the cutting won't destroy us, His pruning shears are instruments of death designed to kill everything in us that's unlike Him. This is so He can release everything He put in us to the world untainted. Yielding to this process means allowing God to use His tools of reaping to shape and prune you into a person capable of producing kingdom wealth. Many are called, but few are chosen in wealth harvesting because few will withstand the process of the Tiller (see Matthew 22:14). God's reaper will strip away all that has the potential to become an idol inside our hearts.

True to the dream, God cut me open for the content of this book. He required me to live it. I felt and endured every single word written on these pages. As I was writing it, I would go through heartbreaking trial after trial and from the midst of pain, God would tell me which chapter to use the pain in.

Long gone are the days of producing from the flesh. These are the days of producing from a place of passion planted by the Husbandman's harrow. People aren't set free with eloquent words on a page and deliverance doesn't take place without the anointing. You will be cut open for this next level. A harvest of wealth cannot be reaped without being cut to the core. It is only when we're cut open and purged that He can use what He put in us. Our feelings become secondary to God's will because His primary concern is that we aren't destroyed by the harvest. Dying in a place where you're called to be fruitful is a tragedy. However, refusing to yield to the cutting process will produce that result.

> *Listen! A farmer went out to plant his seed. While he was planting, some seed fell by the road and the birds came and ate it up. Some seed fell on rocky ground where there wasn't much dirt. That seed grew very fast because the ground was not deep. But when the sun rose, the plants dried up because they did not have deep roots. Some other seed fell among thorny weeds, which grew and choked the good plants. So those plants did not produce a crop. Some other seed fell on good ground and began to grow.*
>
> *Mark 4:3-8a, EXB*

Introduction

There are some who access quick platforms, influence, or wealth but when heat comes, they are destroyed because they have not been cut and their roots are not deep. They've been promoted but not prepared. The seeds fell on unprepared and unplowed ground, so roots could not be developed. Sadly, weeds choke the life out of whatever they lay their hands to. Mark 4: 19 explains it this way:

> *The worries and cares of the world [the distractions of this age with its worldly pleasures], and the deceitfulness [and the false security or glamour]of wealth [or fame], and the passionate desires for all the other things creep in and choke out the world, and it becomes unfruitful.*

This will not be the fate of those called to harvesting kingdom wealth. Anyone operating in this dimension must be first rooted and grounded in God. In doing so, our roots will be so deep that we won't be "blown away" by what this world has to offer. And when the heat comes to test you, "you will be like a tree planted by the water that sends out its roots by the stream, not fearing heat when it comes. Your leaves will always be green" (see Jeremiah 17:8). When you are deeply planted, you'll have the ability to remain surefooted upon your high places while nourishing the earth with your harvest.

> *I assure you and most solemnly say to you, unless a grain of wheat falls into the earth and dies, it remains alone [just one grain, never more]. But if it dies, it produces much grain and yields a harvest.*
>
> *John 12:24*

God gives seed in the form of dreams, then He allows them to fall to the ground and die. He gives us purpose but then allows us to feel hidden and purposeless for a season. He gives us vision only to leave us blindsided by circumstances and blinded to the outcome. God challenges the position of our hearts by killing our finances, jobs, and relationships. He will tear down self-erected mini-kingdoms pieced together with our own two hands of clay. Because in order to produce kingdom wealth, we must first die to earthly agendas. To reap a harvest of wealth, death to the wrong mindsets and motives is inevitable.

> *After you have suffered a little while, the God of all grace [Who imparts His blessing and favor], who called you to His own eternal glory in Christ, will Himself complete, confirm, strengthen, and establish you [making you what you ought to be].*
>
> *1 Peter 5:10*

The VOICE version says God will "restore, strengthen, support and *ground* you." After God tears down and uproots, He builds up and grounds. His goal in destroying our kingdoms is not to embarrass or to hurt us but to complete His kingdom purpose in us. And by the time He's done making us what we "ought to be," we'll be strong and established. We'll be secure in Him and not in wealth, titles, or fame. Trust that the fruit of your suffering will yield a harvest of great blessings.

GOD, THE LORD OF THE HARVEST

If you are called to harvest wealth, you will find that you have a special grace to grow it. Yet the ultimate treasure is not the treasure found inside our wallets or in our bank accounts for only our pleasure. Instead, Jesus unearths a greater purpose in Matthew 9:36-38.

Introduction

When He saw the crowds, He was moved with compassion and pity for them, because they were dispirited and distressed, like sheep without a shepherd. Then He said to His disciples, "The harvest is [indeed] plentiful, but the workers are few. So, pray to the Lord of the harvest to send out workers into His harvest.

The Apostle Paul reveals in Philippians 3 that souls being brought into the knowledge of Jesus Christ is the superior prize; everything else is dung. So, while God needs you wealthy, riches for *your* sake is not *His* only goal. The Lord of the Harvest has heard the bellies of those ordained to His kingdom growling. Their deliverance is tied up in your harvest. Thus, the accumulation of wealth is amassed with the purpose of funding kingdom initiatives and feeding His sheep. There is a harvest of wealth ordained for your life because there is a wealth of souls ordained for His kingdom.

YOUR HARVEST OF WEALTH IS CONNECTED TO A
HARVEST OF SOULS.

This is the season for those whom God has torn and healed, cut, and recovered to rise and serve Him from the depths of their soul with the fullness of their harvest. Song of Solomon 3 speaks of King Solomon being carried on a carriage surrounded by mighty, trained warriors ready to fight for him. The Message version says they were "ready for anything." God is releasing a generation of leaders likened to Solomon who operates in great wealth while reigning in world spheres. He is also releasing skilled warriors of wealth ready to wield riches against the deluge of poverty in the earth. Yes, God has reserved unto

Himself a remnant of believers equipped and ready for anything. They are willing to go forth and bless His people in ways unparalleled.

It's time to prepare for your harvest. It's time for wealth accumulators and generators to emerge. It's time for wealth harvesters to break through and take their rightful positions in the kingdom. It is time to infiltrate world spheres and territories, taking dominion in the tilled good land God has ordained for your life (see Deuteronomy 8:7). It's time for believers to stand in the fullness of authority endowed and entrusted to them by the Lord of the Harvest. It's time to operate in kingdom wealth unashamedly and unapologetically.

The Foundation of Wealth is designed for those called to harvest wealth for God's purposes. The first installation of three, its objective is the laying of a good, Biblical foundation upon which successful businesses, organizations, ministries, visions, and dreams are birthed. This book is a charge for you to grow, evolve, and mature in the place where God specifically planted you. I invite you to come along with me on this journey of self-realization, development, and confirmation. *The Foundation of Wealth* also serves as an instrument to shift mindsets and regulate thoughts by accurately dividing the Word of God as it pertains to riches. It will challenge erroneous religious mindsets as it relates to money. It will ground you in sound knowledge.

There is a plentiful harvest of souls, and you play a vital role in gathering them for the Lord of the Harvest. It is my sincerest prayer that the wealth harvester within you arises not only with wealth in your hands but with the love of Jesus in your heart. I pray that His compassion for the souls attached to your harvest grips you as never before.

PART ONE

A TIME TO BREAK DOWN

1

BEAUTIFUL RUINS

I LOOKED THROUGH PHOTOS taken while visiting Aruba and found myself unimpressed. I skimmed over pictures of the extravagant resort, smiling faces of family members, perfectly arrayed meals, and breathtaking scenery. I looked beyond relaxing photos of the beach that reflected solace and peace. Under normal circumstances—after having spent time on a beautiful island—the memories would have caused me to smile. But this time my heart would not allow it. The truth was, my circumstances were far from what I'd grown to know as normal. And even though I was in a place many would call paradise, and even though I posed vivaciously in photos, walked with flamingos and perused utopia, my heart was overwhelmed. Outwardly, I was in a beautiful place, but inwardly I was ruined. I was in the midst of a heart-wrenching stripping process. God had stripped me of my money, job, perfect credit, car, and even my home. Every day until that point I'd lost something I valued. And every day I wondered if God cared. I found it difficult to trace His footsteps amongst the ashes of my life. I couldn't see Him beyond the wreckage. I couldn't hear Him in demolition's midst. My entire life was in rubble and I was completely devastated.

I continued to scan photos and finally saw one that resonated inside my heart. A picture that was taken during a day-long tour brought revelation that changed my life and my perspective. Allow me to explain. I'll start by saying I abhor "outside" activities. I minimally tolerate beaches. And although I learned to swim in college, because I don't have fins, oceans intimidate me. The thought of camping makes me itch and I've never, ever been a fan of deserts. However, to satiate my family's adventurous appetites, I sacrificed my feelings and climbed aboard a tour bus. Initially, the tour was going quite well. From the confines of a comfortable, air-conditioned bus, I felt safe and relaxed. The bus drove us past gorgeous pristine beaches, million-dollar homes, designer shops, and five-star restaurants. But suddenly the scenery began to change. The same tour bus that drove us through the beautiful sites was now driving us down long, dusty dirt roads. Like most tourists, I continued to smile listening to the driver rehash "funny" antidotes. Yet further and further away from luxury the tour guide continued to drive. He drove until we were in the middle of nowhere, a desert place. And then the bus stopped, and the door opened. It was then I realized I would no longer have the luxury of viewing the desert from the inside, I'd have to experience the heat on the outside. Much to my chagrin, I found myself in a hot, dry, isolated place full of ruins. Moments later, I craved the comforts of the plush resort where I'd sit and remember the experience of the desert rather than experience it.

One of our first stops on the tour was the *Bushiribana Gold Mill Ruins*. Without a tour guide, one would assume that this historic site is merely an unimpressive pile of muted stones. However, in this place of ruins once stood a gold smelter site built in 1872. It is there where Aruba's gold industry gained over 3 million pounds of gold. Gathering the gold seemed simple enough. An old-fashioned grind mill was built to grind the rocks into dust, then powered by the mighty trade wind of the northeast sea, the dust would leave behind clumps of hidden gold. After the clumps were melted, it resulted in pure gold. Though it appeared unlikely, there was once gold found in that place of ruins.

Next on the tour was the *Black Stone Beach*, but this was no ordinary beach. Actually, it really didn't resemble a beach at all. Covered with huge sporadically placed rocks and black sand it appeared as though it'd been blown up. Imagine my shock when I discovered that it had been. This beach was the byproduct of a volcanic eruption which shook the earth beneath the ocean and ripped it up from its normal place. Elements from the ocean's deep were then transplanted into places foreign to it, dry land. Shaken at its very core, it was stripped bare. Stones from beneath were thrown around, however, beautiful natural bridges were formed.

Prior to the explosion, the beach was like every other beach on the island gaining lackluster attention from tourists. To become an above average tourist attraction it had to be torn apart; its natural order had to be upset. It's interesting that the Black Stone Beach only got its edge when it was destroyed.

UNNATURAL BEAUTY IS EXCLUSIVE.

Once the beach lost its pristine attractiveness, it gained a rugged authentic splendor unsurpassed by and unique to any other place in the entire world. This one of a kind beauty could only be accomplished by its ruination. And while the beach was no longer beautiful according to the standards of other beaches, it dawned on me that it was perfectly destroyed. It was beautifully ruined.

I resembled every other person I knew. I blended in with the rest of the community. I was educated, and I worked hard. I grew up in church. I prayed. I fasted. I served. I wore the appropriate "church attire." I knew all the catchphrases and lingo. I could quote a Scripture at the drop of a dime. I followed all the "rules." I was a perfectly average Christian… outwardly. However, when God gets ready to spring up new things on the earth, He doesn't use rehearsed patterns. He sends a wrecking ball to the old to make room for the new (see Isaiah 43:19). He breaks down everything we think we are to bring forth who He knows us to be. God is the Divine Wrecker and Renovator of our lives. Meaning, if we want to be uniquely used by God, we can't blend in with the rest of the world. We will have to be ruined into the perfected version He unearths with the furnace.

*See, I have refined you, though not as silver; I
have tested you in the furnace of affliction.*

Isaiah 48:10, NIV

While I was "fine" outwardly, God needed to refine me
inwardly. Much like the Bushiribana Ruins, God used the
furnace of affliction to bring to the surface all the weeds that
would keep me from pouring forth from a pure vessel. It was in
the midst of the renovation process that my motives erupted
before my eyes.

*And as I watched, the clay vessel in his hands
became flawed and unusable. So the potter
started again with the same clay. He crushed and
squeezed and shaped it into another vessel that
was to his liking. O people of Israel, can I not do
the same to you as this potter has done? You are
like clay in My hands—I will mold you as I see fit.*

Jeremiah 18: 4,6

Even when it appears as though God is ruining your life,
He's not destroying your true self. He's destroying the person
life has caused you to become. Because like me, many of you
have allowed yourself and others to mold you into an unusable
vessel. And you will never pour out what God designed if your
vessel isn't formed "to His liking." He will crush your false life,
the one you've constructed on your own because He sees your
true self. And while He's demolishing the "old you" outwardly,
He's building up the "new you" inwardly. Sooner or later your
inner reality will change your outward circumstances. Isaiah
51:3 promises:

*For the Lord will comfort Zion [in her captivity];
He will comfort all her ruins. And He will make
her wilderness like Eden, and her desert like the*

garden of the Lord; Joy and gladness will be found in her, Thanksgiving and the voice of a melody.

Second Corinthians 1:4 also says God "comforts us in our affliction so we will have the ability to comfort those who are in any kind of affliction." God rarely delivers us immediately from our ruins, but He comforts us in them. And at the appropriate time when He restores you, you will see a version of yourself that's never been seen before. You will find that He has grinded away the rough exterior to release the gold within. You will look in the mirror and see a powerful version that has been buried beneath falsified pristine beauty. You'll see the version capable of comforting others in affliction. The question is, are you willing to be unearthed? I encourage you not to forgo the beauty God desires for a beauty that feels safe and comfortable.

THE REAL YOU IS UNEARTHED WHEN THE OLD
YOU IS RUINED.

In a dream, I stood upon the roof of a high-rise building. Next to that building was an equally high building. Suddenly, the building next to me came crashing down by fire. A large green traffic light fell on it. After witnessing this I ran into the bedroom of the building I stood upon. I sat on the bed and asked two people "why would God allow that to happen?" They could offer me no explanation.

God was revealing what would happen in my life. He was showing me how He would break down every fleshy kingdom I'd ever built. There would be a tearing down of my idols, notions, ideas, plans, and motives. In the days to follow, like clockwork, one by one every idea, every website, every dream, every ministry I'd built crumbled to the ground. And just like the dream, I found myself asking "why is God allowing this to happen in my life." First Corinthians 3:13-15 explains:

> *Each one's work will be clearly shown [for what it is]; for the day [of judgement] will disclose it, because it is to be revealed by fire, and the fire will test the quality and character and worth of each person's work. If any person's work is built [on this foundation, that is of his own effort] remains [and survives the test], he will receive a reward. But if any person's work is burned up [by the test], he will suffer loss [of his reward] yet he himself will be saved but on as [one who has barely escaped] through fire.*

When you are in this fiery process, you will find yourself in need of answers. You'll wonder why God is allowing your life to be ripped up from the place you've grown comfortable in. They may not have an answer for you, but I do. God has to test every work, ministry, business, and organization that we attach His name to. He will try the foundation upon which it stands. If underneath the establishment lies bad character and inadequate quality, He will tear it down. God will send a divine volcanic eruption to shake you at your core to transplant you in a unique place that sets you apart. You will stand upon your high places unmovable and unpolluted. And when you execute your vision, it won't be laced with anger, pride, selfish ambitions, or impure motives. It will be fortified with wisdom from experience. However, gaining that experience is disruptive.

Just as I didn't want to experience the tour's actual ruins on the outside, I didn't want to experience the ruination of my life either. It's easy to give advice from an undemanding place of convenience, but what happens when our cozy place transforms into a desert place? Further, how can we truly help someone out of a fire we've never been in?

> To the weak I became [as the] weak, to win the
> weak. I have become all things to all men, so that
> I may by all means [in any and every way] save
> some [by leading them to faith in Jesus
> Christ]. Who is weak, and I do not feel [his]
> weakness? Who is made to sin, and I am not on
> fire [with sorrow and concern]?
>
> 1 Corinthians 9:22; 2 Corinthians 11:29

Apostle Paul suffered being shipwrecked, endured beatings, experienced hunger, sleep deprivation, conflict, and much criticism. To win the weak, he became weak. Yet, he still gloried and boasted in his trials and found the experience of Jesus worth all he'd lost (see 2 Corinthians 11). Experience changed his perspective.

It is mistakenly believed that Paul's name was changed from Saul, but Scripture does not indicate this. One moment he was called Saul then another he is called Paul with no explanation. I believe Paul was in Saul all along and when he had the experience with Jesus on the Road to Damascus, Paul was called forth. In order to become the vessel of hope and salvation God desired for him to become, he had to become everything those in need of hope and salvation were. To win the meager ones, Saul would be torn from his high place of normalcy and planted in a meager position. Saul was privileged, but Paul would be persecuted. Saul came from the cream of the crop, but Paul would be challenged and ignored. Saul was at the very top according to the world's standards. However, Paul would learn that God's ways were starkly different from the world's. The world teaches us to be "go-getters." It teaches us to "grind" and to force our way into positions at the top. A synonym for "grind" is *slavery*. Galatians 4:7 reminds us that we are no longer slaves, but sons and daughters; we are heirs in His kingdom. This leads me to believe that those operating in grace don't have to grind only be grinded.

> *Brothers and sisters, think of what you were when you were called. Not many of you were wise by human standards; not many were influential; not many were of noble birth. But God chose the foolish things of the world to shame the wise; God chose the weak things of the world to shame the strong.*

> *1 Corinthians 1:26-27*

While the world predicates success upon who we are and what we have, God bases success upon obedience (see Joshua 1:8). This obedience is even unto death; death to everything we think we are entitled to. We must forget about *our* position, *our* influence, *our* name. God is not concerned about the name we've given ourselves, only the one He gives. God has the power to call our true selves forth, and He does so by demolishing us with trials and tribulations.

> *And not only so, but we glory in tribulations also: knowing that tribulation worketh patience; And patience, experience; and experience, hope...*

> *Romans 5:4*

God is raising up wealth harvesters to serve as bridges of hope over troubled waters. But without the experience of suffering, there's not much we can add to anyone else's experience. The experience of tribulations sharpens us in areas we were created to help deliver others from. The experience of endurance not only garners the proven character needed for the next level, but it also commands respect. Because with experience comes wisdom that can't be read in a book or imparted at the will of human hands. I found experience to be the best teacher.

The transparency written in the pages of this book is solely based upon my obedience to God. During the process, there are few that I opened up to about my experiences. To some degree, they walked through the fire with me and shared in my sufferings. This is important because I've learned that there are some who are willing to partake in your season of resurrection but not in your season of crucifixion. This mindset often overlaps into our relationships with Jesus.

> *And this, so that I may know Him [experientially, becoming more thoroughly acquainted with Him, understanding the remarkable wonders of His Person more completely] and [in that same way experience] the power of His resurrection [which overflows and is active in believers], and [that I may share] the fellowship of His sufferings, by being continually conformed [inwardly into His likeness even] to His death [dying as He did].*
>
> *Philippians 3:10*

So often we desire to reign with Jesus but not experience pain with Him. We desire the platform without persecution. We want the favor without the unfavorable tests. We want a place at a table but scorn His cup. We want a crown but no cross.

However, the blessings of the Lord are open invitations to sit at the table of His sufferings. Because it is during this experience of suffering that you finally realize that your only help is the Lord.

I watched my two-year-old niece Cali struggle with a toy chest twice her size. She tried, and she tried to move it but was unsuccessful. Finally, she looks up at me and admits, "I need help. Help me." I quickly arose and picked the toy chest up, but she kept her hands on it. She was trying to help but was only slowing me down. Finally, I told her "take your hands off." She obeyed, and we arrived at her intended destination where she began to build a "burger" with plastic food items. However, she piled so many items incorrectly on the burger that it kept falling down. Again she looks at me and yells, "I need help!" But then she stood in the way of the toy food; I couldn't access it. I finally told her, "you're standing in the way. You've got to move so I can help you."

You've got to take your hands off. You've got to get out of the way. God allowed it to fall so He can build it up the correct way. But He will rebuild us before He rebuilds *it*. Before He can restore *it*, He must restore us into the vessel He envisioned. Also, our motives for building will be purified because if we're not careful, we will become so busy building things for God that we are no longer building anything with Him. "Thy kingdom come, thy will be done," must be engraved upon our hearts. If not, we are merely ambitious souls on a quest to build worthless kingdoms founded upon fleshly efforts. This humanistic reasoning always ends in destruction and confusion. Because any construction built atop what we've erected in the flesh is nothing more than a modern-day tower of Babel (see Genesis 11).

When you find yourself in a low place of ruins looking up for help, allow me to encourage you with what God told me,

"You build in the valley, not from the mountaintop." In the valley you have no choice but to look up. And once you look to the right Source, you'll find the answers needed to build upon a sure foundation. After He has tested you and torn down your structures, He will give the "green light" to build again. He will pick you up, elevate and promote you. Your land of ruins is merely a pathway ushering you into a position of unprecedented grace and favor. Your life may presently look like a pile of wreckage but there is wealth in your ruins.

2

WEALTHY RUINS

I SAT IN MY CAR desperately needing to hear the voice of the Lord. Amid everything I was enduring, I wanted to know that He was still there. I asked Him to speak. Though I heard nothing I felt a refreshing wind blow through my window. It'd been so incredibly hot and humid lately that I immediately took notice. I thanked God for the gentle blowing of the wind. Minutes passed, and I felt myself becoming uneasy as I hadn't gotten word from Him. Suddenly, I felt another refreshing blow of the wind. And again, I thanked Him for the wind. It was an hour later as I drove away despondent that I realized God *had* spoken, I just didn't recognize the way in which He came.

WEALTH IN THE WIND

> *After the earthquake, there was a fire, but the Lord was not in the fire. After the fire, there was a quiet, gentle sound [the sound of a gentle whisper/blowing/wind; or a brief sound of silence; a still small voice].*

> *1 Kings 19:12, EXB*

Elijah, known as "the fiery prophet," accomplished amazing exploits for God. He'd made a fool of false religious leaders, called down fire from heaven, and slain 450 prophets of Baal. But still, Elijah sank deep into a cave of depression. And because he was in such a low and lonely place, the Lord trained his ears to hear Him in a unique and calming way. God spoke by a "gentle blowing" of the wind. I'm sure this approach must've baffled Elijah because he was accustomed to seeing the Lord move in explosive, mighty ways. Yet, the wind was blowing out the fire he was used to. God chose a still, small voice to whisper the instructions needed to steer him out of his low place and into the "mouth of the cave."

> *When Elijah heard it, he pulled his cloak over his face and went out and stood at the mouth of the cave. Then a voice said to him, "What are you doing here, Elijah?"*

> *1 Kings 19:13*

Many of us have retreated into caves of depression in our pursuits of destiny because fear and confusion has settled in. Maybe you've even been feeling ignored by God. Know that the problem is never with God speaking to us, it's with our inability to discern the way He's speaking. The problem is you've been accustomed to hearing God in one way, but He's introducing His wind to train you to hear Him in a new way. Sometimes He answers by fire to show you He's mighty. Sometimes He answers in silence to teach you to trust Him. Sometimes He answers in a whisper to train you in discernment. To navigate the winds of wealth, we must become acquainted with His voice in ways we've never experienced. God is releasing instructions to navigate you to the high place He ordained, but He's using His wind of adversity to do it. It's time to come to the mouth of the cave to hear what the mouth of God is saying.

> *God said to Noah, "I intend to make an end of all that lives, for through men the land is filled with violence; and behold, I am about to destroy them together with the land. Make yourself an ark... This is the way you are to make it... So Noah did this; according to all that God commanded him, that is what he did.*
>
> *Genesis 6:13-14a*

At the age of 535, Noah was commanded to build in a time where sin and degradation ran rampant upon the earth. Needless to say, his exploits did not come without winds of adversity. Noah was to prepare for an unheard of, torrential rain in a place where there had been none. So quite possibly, he built amid opposition and mockery because he was accomplishing something that was unprecedented. Yet when he heard the instruction of the Lord, he obeyed. The ark was constructed according to God's precise measurements.

> *Noah was six hundred years old when the flood (deluge) of water came on the earth [covering all of the land].*
>
> *Genesis 7:6*

Sixty-five years later, as promised the inundating rain came; the whole earth was flooded. I imagine Noah watched as everything around him drowned. There was complete devastation to the world as he knew it. Imagine for a moment being on a ship riding wave upon wave of uncertainty. An experience of this magnitude could've raised many questions and concerns in the hearts of most men. But Noah wasn't most men. God singled him out for this task because his heart was prepared to receive His voice. And what separated Noah from every other man on the earth was his divine instructions from God. His ship was built to navigate to the torrential downpour of rain. And while everything around him was dying, he carried life. From Noah's Ark, humanity would emerge once more. In that ark were souls that would fill the earth, be fruitful and multiply.

RAIN PREPARES US FOR REIGN.

Cali hates thunderstorms. The other day as rain poured from the heavens she told me "to make the rain stop." To appease her, we prayed yet still the rain persisted. "It's not working," she said. Little did Cali know, there was a greater purpose for the rain and God would not stop it because she was uncomfortable with it. The rain watered the earth and caused needed growth.

Great leaders aren't birthed in the calm, resistance and waves are their personal trainers. When you are called to accomplish something unheard of you will experience unheard of opposition. Like Elijah and Noah, God will use the rain in life to prepare us for our reign in life. The only reason Elijah was able to hear the gentle blowing of God's voice was because he was first able to stand through the hurricane and the earthquake sent by God. The same God who sends earth-shattering words of fire sends the wind. God crafted your wind, so you'll become sturdy enough to stand in wealth. On the one hand, rain symbolizes blessings and, on the other it represents judgment. The same wealth meant to bless you can curse you if it's not handled appropriately. Therefore, His voice of instruction is vital. So instead of cowering in a cave, it's time to stand, listen and build.

> *And God remembered and thought kindly of Noah and every living thing and all the animals that were with him in the ark; and God made a wind blow over the land, and the waters receded.*

> *Genesis 8:1*

Five months passed, and God *remembers* Noah. In order for Noah to be remembered, at some point he must have felt forgotten. This is understandable. It's easy to feel forgotten when God has given you a vision and it appears to tarry. It's easy to feel hopeless but though it tarries wait for it, it will not tarry (see Habakkuk 2:3). How could something tarry and not tarry at the same time? It's because we may *think* we know when it's time, but only God truly knows the appointed time. And when God releases His wind, what He promised appears to come immediately. At the perfect time, God's wind pushed back the rain, so Noah could see the land He had reserved. If Noah had stepped out of the boat prematurely he would've drowned in the land he was called to possess.

At one point it seemed I couldn't get over one trial without another one overlapping it. I wondered why God constantly blew His wind of adversity in my life. One day as I thought on the problems I'd been facing, my eyes focused on an oak tree. I thought about its roots and how deep they were spread into the earth beneath. I thought about how that very tree had recently withstood a hurricane and a tornado. Then I thought about the beauty of a potted plant. Though they are great for decorative purposes, the potted plant had no roots in the earth and could never withstand a hurricane. It would fold and break with even the gentlest breeze.

The life of a wealth harvester is no walk in the garden. Your ark must be constructed to navigate the torrents of wealth. Wealth has been known to uproot and drown those who were not built to handle it. Our roots must be spread deep, so we will be spiritually stable, stand firm and be unmovable always abounding in good works (see 1 Corinthians 15:58).

> So that we are no longer children [spiritually immature], tossed back and forth [like ships on a stormy sea] and carried about by every wind of [shifting] doctrine, by the cunning and trickery of [unscrupulous] men, by the deceitful scheming of people ready to do anything [for personal profit].
>
> Ephesians 4:14

God equips us with His wind. He uses it to blow away that with the potential to distract us. There is a false wind blowing, vying for our attention and if we're not careful, we could easily fall for the schemes of the enemy. Your heart must be centered on the will of the Lord. You must be prepared to use your harvest for righteous purposes. Haggai 1:9 says:

> You look for much [harvest], but it comes to little; and even when you bring that home, I blow it away. Why?" says the Lord of hosts. "Because of My house, which lies in ruins while each of you runs to his own house [eager to enjoy it].

The wind of God will blow away every kingdom we attempt to erect for unwholesome purposes. Our concern must be building up His kingdom and not our own. This is important because wealth harvesters will experience wealth like torrential rain. And because there are souls to be saved for the kingdom, it will come suddenly. Only those who been through the rain and have built upon the sure foundation will have the ability to navigate it.

In the 1800's it was determined that ⁵"trade winds" served as beneficial because they blew in one direction and expedited the sailing of ships in route for trading. These winds were conducive to laying hold of great riches. In essence, the wind served as a catalyst to obtain wealth. The term trade winds originally derive from a fourteenth-century word meaning "path," or "track." Isaiah 43:16-17 (NLT) declares:

> *I am the Lord, who opened a way through the waters, making a dry path through the sea. I called forth the mighty army of Egypt with all its chariots and horses. I drew them beneath the waves and they drowned, their lives snuffed out like a smoldering candlestick.*

Until now, your path may have been unclear, and you haven't had the ability to see past the rain, but God is sending a wind to recede the rain, so you will see what the rain produced in the earth. Trade winds are coming to push the rain back to reveal a path that's meant for you to walk along. I'm believing God for winds of clarity to blow through your life. His wind is coming with the force needed to accelerate you to the good land designed for you. The wealth in the wind is blowing in your direction. God is blowing His wind over your ideas. He is blowing His wind over your ministry. He is blowing His wind over your foundation. His mighty wind of wealth is coming for that which has been firmly founded upon His principles and instruction. If found worthy, it will surely stand.

WEALTH IN THE DARK

"It's dark, it's dark, it's dark," exclaimed my niece Cali as she looked up and realized that the light of the sun had faded into the moon. Normally she had time to see the sun going down but this time she looked up and found herself suddenly in the dark. She so feared darkness and would rant about it to anyone who'd listen. That day she chose me and complained until I finally told her "I can't control the darkness, you'll have to speak with God about that."

> *I will give you the treasures of darkness [the hoarded treasures] and hidden wealth of secret places, so that you may know that it is I, The LORD, the God of Israel, who calls you by your name.*
>
> *Isaiah 45:3a*

Dark places are often frightening but unavoidable. There are treasures you cannot access unless you enter a dark, secret place to get it. What is this dark, secret place? In my experience, it is a lovely, horrifying place. It is a place where you grow in your intimacy with God, but you relinquish everything you feel entitled to. It's there where you are anointed and strengthened by your tears (see Psalm 84:5-7). It's where you see God's face, but not His hand. You experience darkness and Light at the same time. He gives you a vision, then takes your sight. It's a place where you go deeper in Him but you're in the dark about your future. You grow in love for Him but hate your circumstances. It is the place where we meet God and face our fears at the same time. In the dark, secret place you learn to trust God and let go of your life. You exchange your life for His. You surrender your planned path for His steps. It is a necessary place where our relationship with Him evolves and we glean wisdom. Yet it's not about us earning wisdom by meeting with God, it's about us being so deeply enthralled in a relationship with Him that His wisdom is a byproduct. You cannot go into the presence of God and leave the same. You leave His presence wiser, stronger, and more equipped. You leave His presence with what's needed to accomplish His will.

Even as I type this book, I am in the dark and it's harrowing. I find it easy to get into the presence of God to thank Him for blessings. It's easy to sit with Him when everything's going my way. But what happens when one moment you're in the light and suddenly you've entered the dark place and you can no longer see Him? What happens when you enter the place where it feels like God has abandoned you and you stumble along your path because you can't feel your way.

> How long, O Lord? Will You forget me forever? How long will You hide Your face from me? How long must I take counsel in my own soul, having sorrow in my heart day after day? How long will my enemy exalt himself and triumph over me? Consider and answer me, O Lord my God; Give light (life) to my eyes, or I will sleep the sleep of death.
>
> *Psalm 13:1-3*

Anger and despondency often set in when you're in the dark place. You're fed up because you know that God could enlighten your eyes if He so desired. So why doesn't He? Why does God choose to keep you in the dark? The riveting story of

Saul on the Road to Damascus in Acts 26:13-14a sheds some light.

> *...I saw on the way a light from heaven surpassing the brightness of the sun, shining all around me and those who were traveling with me. And when we all had fallen to the ground, I heard a voice in the Hebrew dialect (Jewish Aramaic) saying to me, Saul, Saul, why are you persecuting Me?*

For three days, Saul was blinded by the Light he'd experienced on the Road to Damascus. I'm sure Saul thought he was "fine" the way he was. He was at the height of his education, career, and influence when he enters the dark to experience the Light. He was left in the darkness with unanswered questions. How uncomfortable and confusing it must've been for him to have been left sitting in this obscure position in a place foreign to him.

THE LORD BLINDS YOU TO GIVE YOU INSIGHT.

I recently attended an event that started later in the day. I hate driving in the dark, so I left immediately afterward. As the sun slowly faded, I put my glasses on and cautiously stopped at a red light. All of a sudden, a reckless driver ran into me, hitting me head on and fleeing the scene of the crime. As I squinted to see the driver's license plate, I discovered that my glasses must've come off during the impact. What I didn't know was, there was a concerned citizen behind me, who wrote the criminal's plate information. Because he saw what I couldn't, I could give the information to the authorities. But even so, this accident took me to a dark place. Devoid of understanding, I couldn't understand why God allowed it. I felt I was already going through enough. Isaiah 30:20-21 offers enlightenment.

> *Though the Lord gives you the bread of adversity and the water of oppression, yet your Teacher will no longer hide Himself, but your eyes will [constantly] see your Teacher. Your ears will hear a word behind you, "This is the way, walk in it, whenever you turn to the right or to the left. Then He will give you rain for you're the seed with which you sow the ground, and bread [grain] from the produce of the ground, and it will be rich and plentiful.*

Though I was eating the bread of adversity and drinking the water of oppression… though I couldn't see, or understand, there was Someone behind me with all the guidance that I need. There is Someone behind you Who knows it all. Whatever your circumstances are, heaven is backing you. Your tears are captured by God. In fact, they water the seeds that are in the earth. There's a harvest that matches everything you've gone through.

During his bout of darkness, Saul hears the Lord speak.

> *Get up and stand on your feet. I am sending you, to open their [spiritual] eyes so that they may turn from darkness to light and from the power of Satan to God, that they may receive forgiveness from their sins and an inheritance among those who have been sanctified (set apart, made holy) by faith in Me.*

> *Acts 26:16a, 18*

Guilty of persecuting believers and wreaking havoc on countless lives, Saul was blinded by the counsel of his own wisdom. He could physically see, but he was spiritually blind. Because of this, he had to be physically blind, so he could spiritually see. See, while Saul had physical eyesight, Jesus knew he needed spiritual insight. According to the Dictionary of Bible Themes, *insight* is "the spiritual quality that enables a person to appreciate God's mind and will in matters of behavior truth and providence, especially where right perception is not obvious." There were ways that seemed right to Saul, but they would end in death (see Proverbs 14:12). So, by blinding him, Jesus gave Saul the ability to see things through His eyes. It was only after this experience that Paul was transformed and able to fulfill his call of opening the spiritual eyes of others. He couldn't turn people away from darkness he'd never experienced. The Divine Presence of the Lord opened his eyes to his destiny and to those he was called to deliver.

As I write this chapter, one of my favorite childhood movies, [6]*Willie Wonka & the Chocolate Factory* (1971), is on. The winners of the coveted "Golden Ticket" are now climbing aboard a seemingly harmless boat which floated on mounds upon mounds of premium milk chocolate. Suddenly, the boat took them down an unexpected path through a dark tunnel and at an alarming speed. As the participants grew increasingly more frightened, Willie Wonka—familiar with the tunnel—remained unbothered. In fact, as the boat pummeled through the tunnel he sang, "Is it raining? Is it snowing? Is a hurricane a-growing? Not a speck of light is showing. So, the danger must be growing. Are the fires of hell a-glowing? Is the grisly reaper mowing?" As uncertainty and sheer terror gripped the hearts of the participants, Wonka finally yells "Stop!" Abruptly, the boat stops on the other side where he would reveal to them the location of his top-secret workshop. It is in this workshop that

Wonka disclosed secret inventions that had the ability to "change the world." They would've never arrived at the workshop of secrets had they not gone through the dark place. And no matter how much they begged him to stop, Wonka did not change his position until they were on the other side. Their resistance was pointless.

Listen to the Words of Jesus in Acts 26:14b:

> *It is hard for you to kick [repeatedly] against the goads [offering pointless resistance].*

The [7]goad is a traditional farming implement used to guide livestock, which pulls a plow. It is a tool with a long-pointed end used also to round up resistant cattle; it poked them into submission. So Jesus was telling Saul that it was pointless to fight against His tool of chastening. The more he resisted the more he would suffer.

To you I say, stop kicking against the goads! Cease your pointless reasoning because only God determines when your boat stops. Only He dictates when your season of darkness ends. If all we've ever seen is light, we could never relate to someone who's in the dark. It's time for you to stand on your feet. It's time for you to enter into the presence of God for innovative ideas, inventions, strategies, and insight (see Proverbs 8:12). I know it's difficult; I know it's dark and I know that you can't see your way, but in the secret place dwells light that's often blinded by our fear.

> *There is no such thing as darkness with you. The night, to you, is as bright as the day; there's no difference between the two. You even formed every bone in my body when you created me in the secret place, carefully, skillfully shaping me from nothing to something.*
>
> *Psalm 139:12*

God is not intimidated by the dark places in your life. To Him, there is no difference between light and dark because He is Light. He does His best work in secret; He is shaping you into something great. Jesus is the Light that serves as illumination to our paths during the dark times, He's right behind you. You have a divine appointment to glean wisdom and knowledge from The Light of the World to change the world around you. You have an appointment to sit at the feet of the King, so you can fulfill the vision, mission, dream, purpose, and destiny He envisioned for your life.

> *He reveals mysteries from the darkness and brings the deep darkness into light.*

> *Job 12:22*

At the end of *Willie Wonka and the Chocolate Factory*, the film's underdog, Charlie, won because he was able to "pass the tests," inflicted upon him by Wonka. Charlie withstood what the others could not. He was not only the poorest, but the last one to enter the factory initially, yet he inherited the entire kingdom of chocolate. The movie ends with Charlie and Wonka breaking through the glass ceiling then floating in the heavens in a glass elevator.

I don't care what you are enduring know that the first will be last and the last will be first (see Matthew 20:16). Blessed are those who are poor in spirit because they will inherit the kingdom (see Matthew 5:3). There are secrets that the King has reserved only for your ears. There is a place of elevation you will reach and there will be glass ceilings you will break through if you are strong enough to walk through the dark places and pass the tests.

WEALTH IN THE DEEP

In a dream, I danced vivaciously on the ocean's floor. While the imagery God used in this dream was priceless, in the natural, if I were submerged underneath water with no protective gear, I'd die. The dream represents the ability to access deep mysteries. These are secrets revealed by God that can't be discovered on the surface level but only in the deepest places, many refuse to go.

> *Can you search out the deep things of God?*
> *Deeper than Sheol-what can you know.*
>
> *Job 11:7a, 8b*

It is said that there are approximately 771 trillion dollars in sunken treasure waiting to be discovered on the [8]ocean's floor. Ocean waters around the world contain about 20 million tons of gold in them. In fact, in 2015, divers discovered 2,000 gold coins on the ocean's floor off the coast of Caesarea. They only discovered it because the night before, Israel's west coast experienced a violent storm that stirred up the ocean's floor and revealed the wealth.

WEALTH IS UNEARTHED ONCE YOU ARE.

If you are called to kingdom wealth, God will reveal it to you in ways that are unprecedented but unearthing. To obtain this wealth, storms must come to divinely excavate it.

Deuteronomy 33 speaks of the special blessings bestowed upon Joseph. Verses 13-16a (**EXB**) reads:

May the Lord bless their land with the wonderful [or the best fruits from the dew] dew from heaven, with water from the springs [and from the deeps] below, with the best fruits that the sun brings, and with the best fruits that the moon brings [or of the months]. Let the old [ancient] mountains give the finest crops, and let the everlasting hills give the best fruits. Let the full earth [earth and its fullness] give the best fruits and let the Lord who lived in the burning bush [the thorn bush; or Sinai] be pleased.

The territory given to Joseph would be watered by the "dew from above" which speaks of fertility, fruitfulness, and opulence. Inside of Joseph's blessing was productive power and abundance. He was also blessed with the "best fruit from the sun and the moon," which speaks of seemingly unending seasons of fruitfulness. The blessings did not stop there, Joseph was also blessed with the "finest crops from ancient mountains and everlasting hills." Those are blessings of high, lofty places; old money and generational wealth. However, of all the blessings, one in particular stood out to me. Joseph was also blessed with "the blessings of the deep."

The word [9]*deep* is defined as "extending far down from the top or surface as in a pit or a deep valley." Deep is also synonymous with the words "submerged, sunk" and "unfathomable." How is it possible to experience blessings in a low place where you feel submerged? Further, how could the same person be blessed with the blessings of high and lofty places, also be blessed with blessings of deep, low places?

Troubles have come again and again [Deep call to deep], sounding like waterfalls [at the sound of your torrents; waters represent distress;]. Your

waves and your breakers are crashing all around
[pass over] me.

Psalm 42:7, EXB

The blessings of the deep are those that can only be obtained by being cast into a deep place. There are depths in which you must dive to receive them. As a harvester, wealth reserved for you will be accessed in ways in which many can't because they are unable to navigate the deep troubles. "Deep call to deep." Deep mysteries call for deep pain. Deep wealth call for deep difficulties. Deep anointing call for a deep pit.

In a dream, I stood in a deep, dark pit with just enough room for one. There was dirt on my face but as I looked up, I saw the light of day. Suddenly, an endless amount of oil was poured over me. This dream helped when I was in a pit of despair, felt alone, and contemplated ways to kill myself. It encouraged me when I felt there was no end to my pain. It was also in this pit that I looked up to God and He anointed me for what was to come. Read the VOICE version of Psalm 42:7 below:

> *In the roar of Your waterfalls, ancient depths*
> *surge, calling out to the deep. All Your waves*
> *break over me; am I drowning?*

In the deep God's loving voice sounds more like a roar and you feel God's hands breaking you. It's hard to imagine that there is any good in the place where you are immersed... the place where you feel as though you are drowning. But while the deep, sunken place is a pit of unfathomable pain, it's often a place of unfathomable of wealth and blessings. And if we are patient with the process God will teach us how to swim and not float.

I remember crying out to God from the very depths of my heart. As many times before, I'd had enough. I felt as though the pain I was experiencing was cruel and served no purpose other than to embarrass me. In the midst of the cries, the Lord said, "I know you're tired, but I need swimmers, not floaters. I am teaching you how to swim because there are too many floaters in the body of Christ." As I thought about what was said, the image of a person lying lackadaisically on his back in a swimming pool with a floaty tool came to mind. Then came the image of an advanced swimmer in a competition. While floating provides hours upon hours of effortless entertainment, competitive swimming involves diving into deep things. Ezekiel 47:5 reads:

> The man measured about one third of a mile [a thousand] again, but it was now a river that I could not cross. The water had risen too high; it was deep enough for swimming; it was a river that no one could cross.

God brought Ezekiel to the door of the Temple where he was given a profound vision. It was there that he saw water flowing from underneath the right side of the Temple. As the angel measured the water, he led Ezekiel in the midst of it. The water grew deeper and deeper. First, it was ankle deep, then waist deep. Then the water was so deep that it was "deep enough for swimming." There was no other way across other than to swim. The angel led Ezekiel to the bank of the water, so he could see the result of the living water he'd nearly been engulfed by. Everywhere the fresh living water went there were signs of life, fish, vegetation, and trees. Listen to the promise given in verse 12:

All kinds of fruit will grow on both banks of the river. Their leaves will not dry and die [wither] and there will always be fruit on them [their fruit will not fail]. The trees will bear fruit every month, because the water comes from the Temple [sanctuary]. The fruit from the trees will be used for food and their leaves for medicine [healing].

Ezekiel 47:12

God is calling forth a remnant of believers who have laid aside their floating devices. He is calling those who have walked through the ankle deep and the waist deep waters. These are those who have learned how to swim and delve into the deep things. Inside of them flows the Living Water that will bring healing to a parched land that so desperately needs it.

The weight of an elephant ranges from 5,000 to 14,000 pounds. What's surprising is that even with their enormous size, they are able to swim long distances in oceans. In fact, they swim entirely submerged with speed and effortless endurance. How? Their bodies, while huge, gives them great buoyancy. They have built-in navigational tools.

When God gets ready to release elephantine movements in the earth, He will use individuals with the ability to carry weight and navigate the deep at the same time. Those with God imparted navigating tools can produce something in the earth besides side shows and speaking "gigs." For too long leaders have floated along the perimeters of the ocean using the tools of their flesh. Many have been guilty of entrapping people with performances and entertainment. No longer will floaters who tantalize the flesh be promoted above advanced swimmers endued with power. Only those operating from a well of the deep will survive.

The peacock is a beautiful and majestic creature. Its vivid "train'" contains over 200 shimmering feathers. Far from being a shy creature, it has the tendency to flash and show off its multicolored feathers in a crowd. What's interesting is that the peacock's feathers are also communication devices. The feathers make infrasonic sounds—inaudible to the human ear—by shaking them. Their behavior reminds me of the Pharisees in Matthew 23:5. It reads:

> They do all their deeds to be seen by men; for they make phylacteries (tefillin) wide [to make them more conspicuous] and make their tassels long.

The Pharisees did nothing from a pure place. They only desired to be seen as holy by men. They made their prayer boxes extra wide and the tassels on their robes extra-long, so they could be spotted easily. To them, their beautifully adorned appearance equaled godliness. They made the outside clean, but inside were full of "extortion and excess" (see Matthew 23:25).

Like the peacock, the elephant also makes infrasonic sounds, but with its voice. And because it makes the sound with its voice, it can communicate over long distances. The days of shaking a crowd based on outward appearance are coming to an end. God is looking for some elephants who have His voice. Elephants aren't that pretty, and they don't perform, but when they hit the earth they make a sound, a movement. God is looking for some elephants who make movements in the earth. Performances entertain but movements shift environments and systems. God is looking for a people who will rely on His grace, not their colorful grind. This earth needs voices of truth, not beautiful lies.

Genesis 37:9, 24 continues and says:

But Joseph dreamed still another dream and told it to his brothers [as well]. He said, "See here, I have again dreamed a dream, and lo, [this time I saw] eleven stars and the sun and the moon bowed down [in respect] to me!" Then they took him and threw him into the pit. Now the pit was empty; there was no water in it.

Many misfortunes fell upon Joseph, the possessor of the grandiose "blessing of the deep." The very dream that elevated him to a high place first demoted him to an incredibly low place. A dream that lifted him to summits, yanked him to the ocean's floor. From the very heights of his mountaintop of dreams, he sank all the way to the bottom. A dream that put excitement in his heart, broke it. The dream that once put a gleam in his eyes, not only caused tears but years of his life. And a dream that once puffed him up in pride, deflated him down in humility. Ultimately, Joseph obtained the wealth of the deep, but only because he went deep into the pit first. In order to emerge in the palace as prime minister, he had to be submerged in the pit as a prisoner.

In a dream—which I discuss more in Chapter 8—I laid on a table inside a storehouse. God lifted me up toward the ceiling. He spoke and gave me a great promise. After which, He lowered me. Like Joseph, I was given a dream that promised elevation, but the same dream would humble me first. That dream landed me at the bottom of the ocean's deep. But not deep in wealth, fame or fortune as promised. No, I was first engulfed by anguish, uncertainty, and the depths of financial ruin. By then the promise was a wonderful, disturbing dream, that both intrigued and wounded me. I found myself lower than I felt humanly possible to go. I felt a pain I'd never experienced. Yet even in the midst of it all something amazing happened.

The pain and the loss and the failure in that deep place landed me deeper into the arms of my First Love. See, I forgot Him; the dream replaced Him in my heart. I pursued *it* more than I pursued Him. The deep forced me to repent and to turn my heart back to the Giver of the dream I worshipped.

Your promise will humble you before it elevates you. And the things that could cause your chest to expand will first cause your head to bow. Yet, the deep is not a place of despair, but a place of mercy. God could leave us alone in our self-absorbed worlds. Instead, He graciously throws us into the deep where we come face to face with our motives; the issues of our petty hearts surface and drown. I now realize that the dream God put in my heart was never intended to drown me but to teach me how to dance on the ocean's floor without forgetting my Life Preserver. I also realize that the grandiose nature of my call is not so grand. The pain made me more aware of my humanity and my deep need for God. He is my Breath and without Him, I'll drift slowly along the coast of safety with no purpose. Without Him, I float aimlessly in an abyss of pain fueled by pride, regret, circumstances, and defeat. I can only pray that He calls me deeper still so that everything with the potential to drown me, drowns in me.

> *The waters [of the Red Sea] saw You, O God; The waters saw You, they were in anguish; The deeps also trembled. Your way [of escape was through the sea, And Your paths through the great waters, and Your footprints were not traceable.*

> *Psalm 77:16,19*

In a dream, I was on the verge of reaching the surface of an ocean. I saw the hand of God lift me from it. I knew that there was a pit below, but I had already been in the pit. The water I was on the verge of was deep, yet I'd already been through the deep. The deep is intimidated by God and overwhelmed by the sight of Him. The deep obeys God and divides into a path at His command. God will bring you out, but the path isn't around the deep waters; You must go *through* it.

> *If I take the wings of the morning or dwell in the uttermost parts of the sea. Even there shall Your hand lead me, and Your right hand shall hold me.*
>
> *Psalm 139:9-10*

Even if you can't trace His steps in the waters of adversity, God knows exactly where you are. He won't allow you to drown. He won't leave you ruined. He's merely breaking everything off you that has the potential to cause you to lose everything. Even when you can't see above the ocean, rest assured that God can. He knows the path that you take; He is with you. You will break through to the top of the seas. God will lift you up and out the deep once you learn to swim in it.

WEALTH IN THE SEAS

While celebrating my sister's birthday in Tampa, I faced one of the most rigorous bouts of spiritual warfare I'd ever confronted. In this place of torment, I was battling feelings of inadequacy, aloneness, and hopelessness. A voice came and said, "deny God, this is too much, it's not worth it, commit suicide." Even though I recognized the voice—the voice of the enemy—for the first time I entertained it. The warfare was so intense that I'd reached a pivotal point where I'd decide if pursuing God was worth it or if I would finally give up...

Escaping Egypt, the Israelites found themselves between two overwhelming enemies. They were being chased by a relentless opponent, Pharaoh, and then face to face with an otherwise inescapable, endless body of water. They felt there was nowhere to turn. In their limited minds, their situation was hopeless. Instead of projecting faith the Israelites projected their fears onto Moses, questioning his leadership abilities. Exodus 14:11 says:

> *Then they said to Moses, "Because there were no graves in Egypt, have you taken us away to die in the wilderness? Why have you so dealt with us, to bring us up out of Egypt?*

Initially, having already been insecure in his call, I'm sure Moses was off-put by their faithlessness. Can you imagine the immense amount of pressure he was under? I imagine him turning to see the mass of people following him awaiting his leadership, then to the mass of water in front of him. Not only this, but there was also the direct threat of Pharaoh's army relentlessly pursuing them. Moses reached a pivotal point in his walk with God. Would he relent and give ear to the voices calling him a failure or would he trust Him?

> *Moses answered the people, "Do not be afraid. Stand firm and you will see the deliverance the Lord will bring you today. The Egyptians you see today you will never see again. The Lord will fight for you; you need only to be still.*
>
> *Exodus 14:13-14, NIV*

Moses had history with God. He'd forsaken the comforts of Egypt, finding true wealth in suffering for God rather than experiencing the riches of the world (see Hebrews 11:26). He'd seen God revealed in the fire (see Exodus 3) and followed His command. God had proven Himself faithful to Moses and so Moses stood firm in his faith in God. However, I wonder what

Moses expected to happen after he cried out to Him. If I were in Moses's shoes, I'd assume that God would dry the sea up or miraculously cause it to disappear. But Exodus 14:15-16 proves differently.

> *The Lord said to Moses, "Why do you cry to Me? Tell the sons of Israel to move forward [toward the sea]. As for you, lift up your staff and stretch out your hand over the sea and divide it, so that the sons of Israel may go through the middle of the sea on dry land.*

God didn't cause the sea to dry up neither did He cause it to vanish. Instead, He commanded His children to "move toward," the sea. It was only as they walked that God created a pathway *through* the sea before them. He literally made a way out of no way. He made a pathway in a sea of impossibilities. As they escaped through the sea, their brazen enemies followed but drowned in the process. Why? They attempted to enter a path that wasn't designed for them.

Just as Moses was trained to navigate the seas, so will those called to navigate wealth. When you are called to greatness, you will have a profound influence, a great following. You must not only be strong enough to stand against the obvious enemy, but you will also have to conquer your own fears, ignoring the voices of people calling you a failure and questioning your God-given methods. Yet instead of expecting God to cause your trial to disappear, He has given you the authority to move toward and conquer the sea that you so fear.

In the book of Revelation, God's voice is described as "many waters" (see Revelation 14:2). *Waters*, as written there, is translated as [10]*mayhim*. The first letter of mayhim in Hebrew is "mem," which resembles the waves of the sea and means "chaos from the storms of the sea." Mayhim is also the plural of "mah" which means "what, where, how, who, and when" because the Hebrews often feared the sea and saw it as an unknown place.

At times, we float on seas of uncertainty. We question God and we question the storms. We wonder when and how God will deliver us. In sheer confusion, I wept one day as I sat in my car. My life was in uproar and totally out of order. I felt I had nowhere to turn. I had no idea what to do to solve my issues. God spoke to me and said "What looks like confusion to you, is order to Me. In the beginning it looked like chaos, but I was establishing order." Genesis 1:2 in the TLV version says:

> *Now the earth was chaos and waste, darkness was on the surface of the deep, and Ruach Elohim (Holy Spirit) was hovering upon the surface of the water.*

God established order *then* He created man, because if He had created man first, he probably would've been overwhelmed by the works of the Lord. God does His best work in obscurity. He creates His greatest miracles in times when things seem dark, confusing, and chaotic.

In the midst of the warfare, I'd been experiencing in Tampa, something happened. The enemy brought a culmination of my hardships to the forefront of my mind. I rehearsed the losses, the lack, and the heartache. I thought about every single thing God allowed to happen in my life until that point. But instead of crying, I smiled. A sense of awe overcame me as I thought about how beautifully awesome God was. I wasn't oblivious to the pain, yet newfound respect for Him gripped my heart. I admired His relentlessness toward me. No matter how much I wanted Him to deliver me from the sea and no matter how much I kicked and screamed, I would have to walk through it. I realized that through it all He was with me. I felt closer to Him than I'd ever felt before. I respected that God didn't move from His position to make mine comfortable. He wouldn't miraculously cause the seas of my life to disappear. He wouldn't cause the waters to dry up. Instead, He would create a pathway through the seas, so I could learn to trust Him to do it.

God will bring each of you to this point because there is danger in disrespecting His instructions and methods. Moses learned the hard way. In the Book of Numbers, God instructed him to speak to a rock in front of the children of Israel so that the congregation and livestock could have a fresh stream of water. But read below how Moses responds.

> *Then Moses raised his hand [in anger] and with his rod he struck the rock twice [instead of speaking to the rock as the Lord had commanded]. And the water poured out abundantly, and the congregation and their livestock drank [fresh water]. But the Lord said to Moses and Aaron, "Because you have not believed (trusted) Me, to treat Me as holy in the sight of the sons of Israel, you therefore shall not bring this assembly into the land which I have given them.*

> *Numbers 20:11- 12*

Even though Moses led the children of Israel through the wilderness, he wouldn't be allowed into the land of promise. Why? The same Moses that had such great trust and belief in God, esteemed the opinions of men as greater. The same man that once navigated seas couldn't navigate a stream. Some may feel that it was harsh of God to keep Moses out of the promise land. Besides, God requested water, and the rock produced an abundance of it. Yet the issue wasn't about what was produced, but how it was produced. Moses created a stream by operating in his own flesh, devoid of God's command. The same loving God that elevates you is the same equally loving God Who will demote you if you put confidence in your flesh (see Philippians 3:3). It's not about you. It's about the countless lives that need to see Jesus revealed in you.

> *Then you will see and be radiant, and your heart will tremble [with joy] and rejoice because the abundant wealth of the seas will be brought to you, the wealth of the nations will come to you.*
>
> *Isaiah 60:5*

The verse above isn't speaking of material wealth, but a rich harvest of converted souls to be gathered in for the kingdom of God. The Message Version says it this way "a rich harvest of exiles gathered in from the nations." The BRG version says, "the abundance of the sea shall be converted unto thee." There are souls depending upon your ability to remain obedient and complete your assignment. There are lives awaiting your ability to navigate the seas. Whether you stand in front of oceans of wealth or a single stream of income, obedience is required.

WEALTH IN THE FIRE

"I hate you, I hate you, I hate you," yelled Cali, as she pummeled outside the bathroom door where I stood. She was quite angry with me and I'll tell you why. She'd recently embarked upon a coloring book expedition and made a big mess in the living room. In the midst of her "creativity" she'd missed her coloring book a couple of times and had drawn on the rug. Crayon, markers, and coloring book pages were thrown all over the place. However, she'd clarified that she didn't want her mess to be touched. I started cleaning it up anyway and Cali wasn't pleased. So there I stood behind the door laughing at her persistent pointlessness. Finally, she grew tired of fighting the door. There was silence. I advanced toward the door and paused when I heard a tiny, calm knock. I answered, "yes." She echoes a final, meek "I hate you." But I could discern by her voice I'd broken through her anger by ignoring her resistance. It was then that I opened the door where she stood and asked, "why do you hate me today?" She looked up and said, "because you're cleaning up my mess."

> *For God is not an indifferent bystander. He's actively cleaning house, torching all that needs to burn, and he won't quit until it's all cleansed. God himself is Fire!*
>
> *Hebrews 12:29, MSG*

God is good. However, inside of His goodness towards us are trials that would lead us to feel in our emotions that He's not. Because God is a consuming fire, He will torch everything in you that's unlike Him, so you can become the clean vessel He desires for you to be. No matter how much we resist the cleansing, God will continue to clean up our mess. He will continue to use His fire to bring forth every bit of dross. The more we fight, the harder it is for us. It is when we humble ourselves and understand God is God that doors will open. God's fiery love is relentless and if it takes Him striking a match to everything you are to get you to who you should be, He will.

In a dream, I heard "the oven reveals the office." Later that morning as I exited onto the highway I saw a company truck called, "Thermo King." It was then I understood that there would be fiery tests coming my way. Although I was already in a place where I was being tested, I'd be introduced to a side of God that I'd never experienced before. I'd come face to face with the Thermo King.

Amid the fire, I complained to God that what I was experiencing wasn't fair. He replied, "it's not fair, but it's fitting." To be "fair" is to be "equal." A synonym for "fitting" is "just what was ordered or needed." Hebrews 2:10 says:

> For it was fitting for God [that is, an act worthy of His divine nature] that He, for whose sake are all things, and through whom are all things, in bringing many sons to glory, should make the author and founder of their salvation perfect through suffering [bringing to maturity the human experience necessary for Him to be perfectly equipped for His office as High Priest].

We all won't go through the same fire because we aren't all the same. Suffering is not created equal. The temperature of your trials is often determined by the degree of your assignment. There is a fire that God orders to fit every one of His children's needs. Your particular fire prepares and matures you into the position God has specifically for you. "Suffering tests your faith which is more valuable than gold (remember that gold, although it is perishable, is tested by fire) so that if it is found genuine you can receive praise, honor, and glory when Jesus the Anointed, our Liberating King, is revealed at last" (1 Peter 1:7, Voice).

One of the last things that God struck a match to in my life was my apartment. Because I was financially ruined, I was forced to move in with family members. It is a blessing to have a family that's there for you. However, being a very independent person for many years, the experience of living with others was a crushing, humbling experience. I migrated from home to home attempting to find peace in the midst of what I viewed as chaos. One day while moving once again, I looked up and saw all the personal items—that I hadn't given away—outside on the ground in front of my mother's home. As I gathered clothes, shoes, and other items, I witnessed a strength in myself that I didn't know was there. Under normal circumstances that experience would've broken me. Instead, I'd already been broken so much by God that humans couldn't. I stood in shock of my development. Even in the midst of pure humiliation I still hung on to God. I could've broken down in front of my family, but Jesus wouldn't have been revealed in me. Jesus can only be revealed in us once the fire has burned away every idol that opposes Him. As I type, I realize that I craved normalcy, the comforts of my past. But just as God had torched all of my possessions, the familiar version of my life was torched as well. And no matter how much I missed the simplicity of sitting in *my* bed and watching a movie on *my* television in *my* apartment, that version of my life was gone forever. And instead of mourning what was, I look forward to the golden version of myself that is being forged by the fire. And instead of covering up my head every morning dreading sunlight, I look forward to every day being the potential day that God's fire has had its perfect work in me.

Is *it* more valuable to you than God? Is your money your protector? God will drown it. Is your trust in your job? The wind of God will carry it away. Is your bank account where you put your trust? He will roast it by fire. Anything that attempts to take God's place in your heart will be ruined. But I encourage you to stop mourning what has been lost in the fire and look forward to what the fire is producing in you. Isaiah 61:3-4 promises:

To console those who mourn in Zion, to give them beauty for ashes, the oil of joy for mourning, the garment of praise for the spirit of heaviness; that they may be called trees of righteousness, the planting of the Lord, that He might be glorified. And they shall rebuild the old ruins, they shall raise up the former desolations, and they shall repair the ruined cities. The desolations of many generations.

A week later Cali looked up from yet another pile of mess and said, "I need help." "With what?" I asked. "I need help cleaning up my mess." As I helped her she also picked up items from the floor but saw nowhere to store them. Lifting the items up towards me, "where can I put this?" she asked. I told her to put it in my hands.

Put your ruins in God's hands. Allow Him to cleanse you, build you, and make something beautiful and wealthy from the ashes.

3

DEATH VALLEY

NEEDLESS TO SAY, THE Apostle Paul was blessed, and he was gifted. He received great and surpassing revelation from the Lord. However, it is important to remember that along with his gift came a tormenting "thorn" to pummel him (see 2 Corinthians 12:7). To be clear, this thorn was no cute little prick. It is translated as being a "stake driven through the flesh." This thorn in Paul's flesh served as an instrument of death. It was a divinely permitted satanic tool of suffering, humiliation, and pain. Because of the inundation of extraordinary revelation Paul's spirit received from heaven, the thorn was a necessary device for his flesh on earth. Every time his flesh desired to rise in arrogance, the thorn stabbed the desire in him to death (see 2 Corinthians 2:7). The pain reminded Paul of his humanity and desperate need for God. God allowed it, so he'd remember to depend on the Source of the gift and that nothing of value could be produced by his vulnerable flesh. The pain caused him to serve from a place of humility.

Those called to a greater measure—whether it's revelation, wealth, wisdom, or power—will be buffeted into submission. Because with great resources comes the great potential to depend on them. And if we get to the place where the gift is valued as greater than the Gift Giver, we have begun to operate in the flesh. The thorn is a necessary evil used as a catalyst to stab our flesh to death.

Philippians 1:21-24 (NLT) says:

> *For me, living means living for Christ and dying is even better. But if I live, I can do more fruitful work for Christ. So really, I don't know which is better. I am torn between two desires; I long to go and be with Christ, which would be far better for me. But for your sakes, it is better that I continue to live.*

What a powerful statement of dedication to a God that allowed him to suffer! No matter how gifted Paul was, he found it a far better option to leave it all behind to spend eternity with Jesus. Yet Paul also realized that his suffering neither the revelation he received was about him. He knew it was about the fruitfulness God desired to release in the earth through him. So while he'd rather depart life to be with the Lord, he understood it was advantageous for souls that he remained on earth and fulfilled his purpose. He found it best to die to his desires by dying to his flesh and living for Christ.

Galatians 2:20 says:

> *I have been crucified with Christ [that is, in Him*
> *I have shared His crucifixion]; it is no longer I*
> *who live, but Christ lives in me. The life I now live*
> *in the body I live by faith [by adhering to, relying*
> *on, and completely trusting] in the Son of God,*
> *who loved me and gave Himself up for me.*

Crucifixion was not only a means of an excruciating death, but it also served as a device of humiliation. The cross, also called a stake, was often elevated on a hill so spectators could witness the brutality inflicted upon its subjects. Jesus experienced one of the most horrific deaths to have ever been witnessed. But what they did not know is that they could not take His life because He had already freely given it before the foundations of the earth (see Revelation 13:8). Second Corinthians 5:15 says:

> *He died for all, so that all those who live would*
> *no longer live for themselves, but for Him who*
> *died and was raised for their sake.*

Because of Jesus, we most likely won't endure a physical cross, but we each must have our own death experience. Aside from physical death, as Christians, we are called to die to our flesh. Jesus died so He could live through us. But He can't live through us if our flesh is constantly on the scene. As a remedy, we will each walk through our own customized "valley of the shadow of death" that will leave us so empty of ourselves that our hearts will honestly profess "to die is gain." As humiliating as the experience is, the humiliation breeds humility. Because in this death walk, there will be an assassination of wrong motives, bad character, evil desires, and self-dependence. Jesus came to earth, conquered death, hell, and the grave, but we must allow Him to conquer our flesh before He can be revealed in us to others.

> *Whoever is not willing to carry the [does not take up his] cross and follow me is not worthy of me.*

Matthew 10:38

You're not worthy to live in Jesus' glory if you can't die to yours. We're not worthy of fellowship at His table if we have no desire to drink from the cup of His suffering. We love His resurrection, but He never would've gotten up unless He first went down. To live for Him, we must die with Him (see Romans 6:8). Stop running from persecution and embrace it. Know that everything you're stripped of physically is being multiplied spiritually in your life.

By nature, I am an enterprising person. Early on, I earned a bachelor's *and* a master's degree to secure *my* future. Shortly after graduating, I landed a job in healthcare for twenty-two years. I prided myself in my resourcefulness and innate ability to take care of myself. I paid my bills, I tithed, I helped others… I detested asking for help; It made me feel vulnerable. It made me feel like less than the independent woman I'd evolved into over the years. Year after year, I continued to build upon my kingdom of material possessions, pride, and self-reliance. Honestly, I served God but had no reason to consult with Him. If I needed something, I wrote a check. When the call to ministry came, I was equally self-reliant. I wrote checks, and obtained a website, business checking account, headshots, and social media accounts. Before I knew it, I'd built an entire ministry given by God, without God. I saw no fruit. Why? I depended on my intellect, resources, and talent to accomplish God's will. But 1 Corinthians 3:7 reminded me that:

Death Valley

*The one who plants is not anybody special, nor
the one who waters, for God is the one who brings
the supernatural growth.*

When God told me to resign from my position, I found it confusing because I had no backup plan. I had no 401 K; I had no savings, I barely had anything in my checking account. But still after months of bargaining, I "stepped out on faith" into the unknown. I trusted God. And because I trusted Him, I expected Him to promote me instantly to the position of favor and increase that was promised. I was wrong. Little did I know I'd enter one of the hottest seasons I'd ever experienced. Little did I know I would be inducted into another process I call "Death Valley."

Located in Eastern California, [11]the Death *Valley Furnace Creek* holds the record for having the highest recorded natural ground surface temperature on earth at 201-degree Fahrenheit. It is described as the lowest point in North America and considered "rock bottom." The valley is long and is 282 feet below sea level, yet it's surrounded by mountains and devoid of plants and vegetation. It's called "Death Valley" because its extreme temperature has caused many deaths in the past.

When God calls you to high places, you will hit rock bottom first. You will experience God's Death Valley. It is a place where there is no evidence of fruit in your life. In fact, it is a place where you are surrounded by mountainous issues that seem insurmountable. It is a devastatingly hot and low place where there's nothing left. Money, people, and things have all dried up. It is the place where you wonder if God wants you dead. Then you realize the answer is yes. He does want you dead; dead to yourself.

Those who belong to Christ Jesus have crucified their own sinful selves [the sinful nature; the flesh].They have given up their old selfish feelings and the evil things they wanted to do [its passions and desires].

Galatians 5:24

I hit rock bottom in Death Valley. And just when I thought it was over, Death Valley introduced fiery trials in my life over and over again. I felt abandoned; I felt ashamed. I felt betrayed. God didn't tell me that I'd first have to catch hell before I'd ever see a glimpse of heaven. One day I'd had enough. I went down a list reminding God of what I'd given up for Him. I felt I had nothing left to give. I cried out and asked Him what else He could possibly want. He said, "your heart."

But once she has nothing, I'll be able to get through to her. I'll entice her and lead her out into the wilderness where we can be alone, and I'll speak right to her heart and try to win her back. And then I'll give her back her vineyards; I'll turn the valley of Achor, that "Valley of Trouble," into a gateway of hope.

Hosea 2:14-15, VOICE

In my quest to fulfill *my* purpose for God, I lost my passion for Him. There were things in me that had to be crucified. I depended on my flesh; I was a peacock. I could entice and perform but hadn't tapped into the level of authority and power God needed me to have for purpose. He took me completely off the scene. I had no ministry engagements; I had no book signings. I felt like a failure and wanted to be visible, but God needed an elephant. So, He led me into the wilderness to smoke the peacock out of me.

Death Valley

When what we own—our jobs, relationships, ministry, bank accounts, destiny—has a louder voice than Who we serve it will dry up. When our wealth has a greater influence than the voice of God, it will wither away. God will dehydrate everything in our lives until He gets us to the place where our hearts thirst only for Him. He will leave Himself as the only option to get us back to the place where we first met Him. You know, the place where you'd spend endless hours talking to Him, praying, and seeking His face. It's the place where He was the most important thing. No matter how uncomfortable and hot this place is God will not relent until our hearts fully belong to Him.

> *Concerning this I pleaded with the Lord three times that it might leave me; but He said to me "My grace is sufficient for you [My lovingkindness and My mercy are more than enough—always available—regardless of the situation; for [My] power is being perfected [and is completed and shows itself most effectively] in [your] weakness.*

> *2 Corinthians 12:8-9*

Apostle Paul, the man with deep revelation from God grew tired of his thorn and asked for it to be removed three times. God denied each of his requests. But He did not deny them because He enjoyed seeing Paul suffer. He allowed the messenger because the suffering was perfecting him. It kept the peacock at bay. And in the midst of Paul's buffeting, he would understand that we are not "sufficiently qualified in ourselves to claim anything as coming from us, but our sufficiency and qualifications come from God" (see 2 Corinthians 3:5).

God led me into the *Valley of Trouble* for my own good, but I experienced things that caused me to despise daybreak. However, in the midst of my loss, I discovered that the suffering is not about me. It's about the movement I'm carrying. It's about the souls attached to my obedience. It's about Him. My heart's desire is to please Him; it pleases Him to have you. And if I have to die so that you gain, that's a sacrifice I'm willing to make. Does my heart ache? Tremendously. Will I stop? Never.

DEATH VALLEY LEADS TO LIFE.

You may be walking through your own Valley of Trouble and feel as though you're losing at every turn. It's necessary. During my Death Valley experience, God said, "to lose is to gain." When we lose physical things, we gain spiritual weapons. When God cuts you, you can't be cut down by the world, you gain strength. When God dehydrates you, you won't be thirsty for attention. When God ruins you, this world can't. When you die to your flesh, you will die to the things of the world. God cares more about you than He does your possessions. He cares more about your heart than what He called you to do. He knows that if we're prematurely positioned behind podiums that don't match our character, it will crush us. So He is coming for everything with the potential to burn you alive.

In a dream, I watched a minister on a large platform singing the lyrics to a song I've never heard before, "Jesus what You're doing is beginning to unfold." He followed by saying, "If you've never gone through anything, you can't go anywhere. I've been through the fire, God has well-watered my strength." This reminds me of a Scripture written in the book of Isaiah. It says:

> *The Lord will guide you always; he will satisfy your needs in a sun-scorched land and will strengthen your frame. You will be like a well-*

watered garden, like a spring whose waters never fail. Your people will rebuild the ancient ruins and will raise up the age-old foundations; you will be called Repairer of Broken Walls, Restorer of Streets with Dwellings.

Isaiah 58:11-12

The scorched earth policy is a military strategy of burning and destroying crops, houses, factories, or any other resources that might be of use to an invading enemy force. The enemy of your soul is roaming the earth seeking to devour you (see 1 Peter 5:8). So, the Lord uses His fire to burn away everything in you that has the potential to give place to the enemy. God will allow everything to be destroyed to see what's inside you. If there's anger in your heart, fire will blaze it to the forefront, it has to burn. If there's greed, it has to be exposed and overcome. If there's independence aside from God, He will torch your finances. Those things must dry out, so He can fill you with His anointing. You can't be full of yourself and full of Him. However, God promises to keep you during the process. He also promises restoration if you are able to withstand the heat of the valley. Psalm 23:4 (MSG) says:

Even when the way goes through Death Valley,
I'm not afraid when you walk by my side.

It was in Death Valley that I lost what I thought had value but gained what was invaluable. I lost stuff, but I gained Christ. I lost my idols of silver and gold, and I gained a deeper respect and intensity for His heart. And God was faithful to protect me.

Hosea 13:5 says:

I cared for you in the wilderness, in the land of burning heat.

The Hebrew word for wilderness is [12]*midbar*. *Midbar* translates as "speak." Though the wilderness is a place of drought, it is not without the voice of God. There is revelation given and impartations received in desert places. There are things that God will speak to you in the valley that you can't receive on the mountaintop. *Midbar* is also translated as a "place of order." So, the wilderness is not only a place where God speaks and gives divine downloads of destiny, but He also repositions you. It is a dry place where everything's gone so there are no distractions. He has free rein to put your life in order according to His original plan.

The anointing on my life didn't come from a church service or from a world-renowned pastor laying hands on me. It did not come from sowing a seed. It did not come from a mentor. It came from my tears. "Sorrow is better than laughter, for sadness has a refining influence on us" (Ecclesiastes 7:3). It was the pain I experienced in Death Valley that increased God's anointing in my life. Every time I cried but trusted Him in the midst of the fire, the Messiah (the Anointed One) touched me. When I felt trapped and alone and there was no one to deliver me, I depended upon the Messiah to pull me through.

THE WILDERNESS IS THE LAND OF REVELATION.

Shadrach, Meshach, and Abednego disobeyed the king by refusing to bow down to his graven image. As a result, they were reprimanded and thrown into a fiery furnace. They were literally on fire for God. Daniel 3:27 says:

> *Then the high officers, officials, governors, and advisers crowded around them and saw that the*

fire had not touched them. Not a hair on their heads was singed, and their clothing was not scorched. They didn't even smell of smoke!

Even though they were in a heated situation, they knew Who controlled the temperature gauge. Even though they walked through the Valley of the Shadow of Death, they feared no evil. Because of their fearlessness, as they stood in their positions of faith, Nebuchadnezzar saw something strange. Jesus was revealed in the fire. What's interesting is that even though they were in a fire seven times hotter than normal, they came out scorch-free; it was as if they were never on fire at all. The fire that you are going through will not burn you alive, but it will forge an unquenchable fire within. You can't be on fire for God until you've been on fire for God. The three Hebrew men were rescued speedily but what happens when it feels like God doesn't deliver you as quickly? Jonah 4:6-8 reads:

> *So the Lord God prepared a plant and it grew up over Jonah, to be a shade over his head to spare him from discomfort. And Jonah was extremely happy about [the protection of] the plant. But God prepared a worm when morning dawned the next day, and it attacked the plant and it withered. When the sun came up God prepared a scorching east wind, and the sun beat down on Jonah's head so that he fainted, and he wished to die, and said, "It is better for me to die than to live."*

Words are easy to speak when you're speaking them from underneath a shade tree in between sips of iced tea. But what comes to the surface when God removes your shade and the heat blazes upon your head? What happens when you are no longer singing praises to His name between breezes in a lush garden? What happens when you're dry, barren, alone, angry, confused, or depressed? What will your heart scream then? He will test you on that. God wants to see if you'll still say He's God even when everything around you says that He's not. When the enemy whispers in the driest place of your life "where is your God," can you whisper back "I know He can deliver me, but even if He doesn't He's still able," (see Daniel 3:18). When the fire is on your back, can you still say, "He's still good?" And even if you "walk through the valley of the shadow of death," will you remember He's still there? Will you know that the same God who prepared the shade tree also prepared the worm to wither it and the scorching wind to burn you?

Even at rock bottom, I landed on the Rock. I found Him to be a faithful Help in times of need. So, there is nothing in this world I need more than Him. He outshines diamonds and out glistens gold. Though it hurts, there's no place I'd rather be than where He wants me to be. There's no platform I desire to mount if He's not there. There's no company I desire to keep unless He ordained the relationship. There is no one and nothing greater; there is no price steep enough to cause me to lose Him and gain this world because He is my world. Is He yours? If not, before you're extradited from Death Valley, He will be.

May the declaration of our hearts match the profession of our mouths and if they don't may God scorch everything moving in and around us until it does.

4

THE HARVESTING BLUEPRINT

MANY REHEARSE THE DETAILS of Joseph's life almost effortlessly. We know him as the dreamer and as the interpreter of the dreams of others. We've heard that his life was interrupted because of his brother's jealousy and hostility toward his destiny. We know how his dreams finally manifested. He was promoted from the dungeon to the dynasty as prime minister, second only to Pharaoh. Yet—often in our haste—we extradite Joseph from the prison to the palace to the grave. In doing so, we often neglect what his role as prime minister entailed. Few acknowledge Joseph as the man who single-handedly defeated poverty in the time in which he lived. Few recognize him as the innovator of the wealth harvesting model that accumulated crops and filled the impoverished bellies of the multitudes. There is much revelation to glean from his responsibilities. Let us start at the beginning. Genesis 37:3-4 says:

> *Now Israel (Jacob) loved Joseph more than all his children, because he was the son of his old age; and he made him a [distinctive] multicolored tunic. His brothers saw that their father loved Joseph more than all of his brothers; so, they hated him and could not [find it within themselves to] speak to him on friendly terms.*

Because Jacob handpicked and favored Joseph, envy filled the hearts of his brothers. The verses above reveal that even before he was despised by his brothers because of his dreams, he was loathed because of the special multicolored robe given to him by his father. When the brilliantly arrayed mantle was worn, Joseph stood out from his brothers. In fact, I'm certain that this vibrant tunic caused him to stand out from most of the surrounding population as well. Imagine for a moment the degree of upset that this distinction must've caused. Delving deeper, I wonder whether the jealousy ignited in the hearts of his brothers was not only because of the robe. Perhaps his brothers knew what the robe represented long before Joseph divulged his dreams. Maybe they sensed that it was symbolic of something more.

Further research gives insight as to what Joseph's robe symbolized and why his brothers were so hostile towards him. The Septuagint reveals that the robe is described as having many "manifold" colors. The word *manifold* is used in Ephesians 3:9-12 (KJV). It says:

- 70 -

And to make all men see what is the fellowship of the mystery, which from the beginning of the world hath been hid in God, who created all things by Jesus Christ: To the intent that now unto the principalities and powers in heavenly places might be known by the church the manifold wisdom of God, according to the eternal purpose which he purposed in Christ Jesus our Lord: in whom we have access with confidence by faith of Him.

The Greek word for *manifold* as used in the verse above is [13]*polupoikilos*, which means "much variegated" or "marked by a diversity of colors," as in a cloth or painting. It suggests that the wisdom of God is rich and endlessly diversified. His wisdom is forever unfolding. No matter what angle you look at His wisdom from, there is always new truth to be found. For example, have you read the same Scripture multiple times and each time received different revelation? God has varied mysteries hidden until He uncovers it. Personally speaking, I've discovered multiple interpretations for a single dream during different seasons of my life.

GOD'S WORD IS FOREVER UNFOLDING.

Manifold also means "multiplication," and "variety." This is interesting as one of the synonyms for wealth is *variety*. This could suggest that while wealth is most certainly a variety of material resources, it also embodies an abundance of spiritual resources to accompany the abundance of physical wealth. Further, the word *variegated* suggests that the wisdom of God is "patterned" or "knit." Psalm 139:13 in the VOICE version says:

*For You shaped me, inside and out. You knitted
me together in my mother's womb long before I
took my first breath.*

The mantle given to Joseph by his earthly father was merely representative of the wealth of manifold wisdom imparted to him by his heavenly Father before the foundations of this earth.

It is the same with us. Even before a person breathes his very first breath, the multifaceted wisdom of God examines the vessel He molded. He then imparts to that individual a wealth of spiritual resources and releases the grace needed to navigate distinctive calls. And because His wisdom is manifold, a thousand people can be called to accomplish the same goal in the exact same sphere and it still looks completely different each time. Ten people can preach a sermon with the same title and each time different revelation is given and received.

Genesis 37: 6-7 continues:

> *"Please listen to [the details of] this dream which
> I have dreamed; we [brothers] were binding
> sheaves [of grain stalks] in the field, and lo, my
> sheaf [suddenly] got up and stood
> upright and remained standing; and behold, your
> sheaves stood all around my sheaf and bowed
> down [in respect]."*

The symbols God used in Joseph's dream—the field and the sheaves—gave insight into how his promotion would come. A sheaf is a bundle of wheat that's been bound together after reaping and harvesting. As discussed earlier, a harvest does not come without reaping. So, before Joseph would see the manifestation of his dreams, he himself would be cut to the core. The field represents the souls that Joseph would bless with his harvest (see Matthew 9:38). This dream served as confirmation of the manifold mantle of wealth harvesting released upon him by God. Joseph's brothers interpreted his dream and discerned his inevitable elevation and promotion above them.

> *They said to one another, "Look, here comes this dreamer. Now then, come and let us kill him and throw him into one of the pits (cisterns, underground water storage); then we will say [to our father], 'A wild animal killed and devoured him'; and we shall see what will become of his dreams!"*

> *Genesis 37: 19-20*

His brothers thought that by stripping Joseph of his robe, they'd also strip him of his elevation. They thought by burying him in a pit, they'd bury his purpose. What they failed to realize is the call of God is irrevocable and human beings don't have the power to strip it away.

THEY THOUGHT THEY WERE BURYING YOU BUT
GOD WAS PLANTING YOU.

When God first called me, I sought "wise" counsel (see Proverbs 19:20). Sadly, I learned that not all counsel was created equal; not all counsel is wise. When leadership ostracized and attacked me, I was in awe. These were people I respected as authentic leaders of God. It was there I learned that people can be more jealous of your potential than who you presently are. I hated confrontation, so I ran from the conflict and joined a different church. I learned, however, that while I could run from men, I couldn't run from God. Everywhere I went, I encountered that same jealous spirit until I conquered it.

Wealth harvesters are endowed with wisdom that is often unique to that of their brethren. This wisdom gives you an inventive edge above your peers. However, because of the distinctiveness, it has the potential to evoke attention and envy. First Peter 4:10 says:

> *As each one has received a gift, minister it to one another, as good stewards of the manifold grace of God.*

The Amplified Version says that God's "multifaceted" grace is given to Christians in diverse and *varied* ways. As stated earlier, everyone called according to God's purposes have been imparted a wealth of wisdom to accomplish great exploits for His kingdom. Yet some gifts will be more visible than others. Harvesters of wealth must remember that though the imparted wisdom is different from your brothers and sisters in Christ, it is by no means superior. It only means that you have a greater capacity for suffering.

> *In all this you greatly rejoice, though now for a little while you may have had to suffer grief in all kinds of trials.*
>
> *1 Peter 1:6*

The words "all kinds" of trials used above is translated as *poikos*, which again means *manifold*. In essence, Joseph's varied manifold destiny came with varied manifold trials. He would see his grandiose dreams manifested but would also learn that increased blessings call for increased capacity. He would be stretched so the wealth inside of him could handle the wealth and responsibility God intended to release outside of him.

> *Enlarge the site of your tent [to make room for more children]; Stretch out the curtains of your*

dwellings do not spare them; Lengthen your tent ropes and make your pegs (stakes) firm [in the ground].

Isaiah 54:2

I once viewed stretching at the gym as a painful waste of time until I discovered its added benefits. Stretching is the intentional lengthening of the body to increase flexibility and range of motion. Stretching warms the body up and prepares it for the rigorous activities ahead; it prevents injuries. Stretching forces us into positions we never thought we could handle. It involves being taken to a place that you believe is beyond your threshold of pain; a place outside of your comfort zone. The stretching hurts and feels unnecessary, but it is.

God's stretching leads to increased capacity. It's necessary because what He desires to pour out of you must first be held. Like Joseph, He will stretch you to enlarge the territory inside to match the territory He releases outside of you. Stretching prepares us to carry the weight of the assignment. It brings the "range" or the "variety" out of us. Stretching enables us to operate at our God-designed capacities. And more importantly, the stretching of God prevents us from causing injury to the body of Christ by straightening out the kinks in our flesh *before* we are placed onto platforms.

STRETCHING MAKES ROOM FOR PURPOSE.

Caveat, it is important never to compare or copy assignments. It is dangerous to boast beyond or step outside your territory. Because along with multicolored assignments comes multifaceted warfare, devils, and trials to match. It may appear easy to mimic what others are doing, but what happens when their devils and hardships seek you out? You can only hold and release what you've been stretched to carry.

Genesis 37:8 continues:

> *His brothers said to him, are you really going to rule and govern us as your subjects?" So, they hated him even more for [telling them about] his dreams and for his [arrogant] words.*

I once believed that Joseph should have been silent about his dreams. Perhaps then he could have avoided the trials he endured. However, I have now come to realize that whether Joseph mentioned the dreams or not, the issues of his heart would have eventually manifested. Arrogance would have to be processed out of him. Psalm 105:19 says, "until the time that his word [of prophecy regarding his brothers] came true, the word of the Lord tested *and* refined him." The word tested as used here is *tsaraph* which means "to purge gold and silver by fire," and "to remove dross or impurities." Joseph would have to be purged and stretched beyond belief to have the attributes needed to compliment the assignment. The weeds would have to be removed. He was called to a position of respect, authority, and wealth, but he could not stand in God as long as he stood in arrogance. Consequently, Joseph was cast into the pit and prison to endure years of rigorous testing and training.

> *Then Pharaoh sent and called for Joseph, and they hurriedly brought him out of the dungeon.*
>
> *Genesis 41:14a*

Though Joseph spent years of his life imprisoned, Pharaoh "hurriedly," brought him out of the dungeon. God simply gave

Pharaoh a dream that only Joseph could interpret and immediately he was remembered. Because after years of pulling and stretching and pain, a need in the kingdom arose that matched the newfound capacity and gifts of Joseph. Once his character aligned with God's assignment, he could be trusted to fulfill destiny.

The gift of God makes room for us, but He will make room in us first (see Proverbs 18:16). God will not release us until our character and gift match His need in the earth. Our time in the pit is not so much about the assignment as it is our alignment. Read the epic display of Joseph's maturity in Genesis 41:15-16:

> *Pharaoh said to Joseph, "I have dreamed a dream, and there is no one who can interpret it; and I have heard it said about you that you can understand a dream and interpret it. Joseph answered Pharaoh, "It is not in me [to interpret the dream]; God [not I] will give Pharaoh a favorable answer [through me]."*

Clearly, the stretching process completed a perfect work in Joseph's life. And instead of arrogance, he displayed humility in grace. He truthfully proclaimed that the wisdom he had didn't originate with him, but it originated with the Highest Power. Joseph understood that while there were mysteries and secrets revealed to him, they came at a high price; a price he didn't want to pay again by laying claim to what only belonged to God.

From experience, I know that the pit will humble you. In it, you will gain the ability to sympathize with those you are called to nourish. Every pit experience is hand-crafted by God and designed to bring forth the passion needed to serve those in your sphere. Does your heart break for the impoverished? Does your heart echo the hunger of the Lord of the Harvest for souls? If not, no worries. By the time God delivers you from the pit, it will. You will emerge with His passion for the impoverished in your heart. Your prayers will evolve; you'll no longer selfishly pray only for your own desires. The desires of God will overtake you and you'll cry out from a place of depth, power, and authority.

THE INFRASTRUCTURE OF JOSEPH

Then Joseph said to Pharaoh, "The [two] dreams are one [and the same and have one interpretation]; God has shown Pharaoh what He is about to do. The seven good cows are seven years, and the seven good ears are seven years; the [two] dreams are one [and the same]. The seven thin and ugly cows that came up after them are seven years; and also the seven thin ears, dried up and scorched by the east wind, they are seven years of famine and hunger.

Genesis 41:25-27

Pharaoh's dreams, interpreted by Joseph, foretold the economic state of the country. It would mean that the economy of Egypt would encounter seven good years followed by seven bad years. After which, Joseph suggested a divine, detailed plan. Pharaoh was impressed. Described as "wise and discerning," he appointed Joseph as prime minister, second in command over his entire palace. Thirteen years after his imprisonment, Joseph's dreams finally fully manifested, and his work immediately ensued. There would be no time for Joseph to gain the needed capacity overnight. He needed the lengthy process beforehand because his reign began quickly. He would institute an infrastructure of store housing that would serve as a blueprint for all wealth harvesting models to follow.

While Joseph gleaned knowledge from officials in the land in Pharaoh's kingdom (see Genesis 41:46), the wisdom that he released to Pharaoh was only by the Spirit of God. If we look over his life, we won't find that he was given courses in economics or agriculture. Joseph's brilliance in the execution of this strategy was not because of his college degree or extensive background. His success was due to a dream coupled with a pit experience and manifold imparted wisdom from God. Joseph's gift as a dream interpreter transposes to that of a financial genius because of his stretched capacity. It enabled him to hold an entire infrastructure of wealth. He was given a greater measure because he could hold a greater measure. The manifold, varied mantle of God was on full display in his life.

> *During the seven years of abundance the land produced plentifully. Joseph collected all the food produced in those seven years of abundance in Egypt and stored it in the cities. In each city he put the food grown in the fields surrounding it. Joseph stored up huge quantities of grain, like the sand of the sea; it was so much that he stopped keeping records because it was beyond measure.*
>
> *Genesis 41:47-49*

As planned, Joseph stored up crops during the seven good years to prepare to feed the famished during the seven bad years. The storehouse groundwork produced so much abundance that it was immeasurable. And by the time the famine reached the earth, the Egyptians were instructed by Pharaoh to "go to Joseph and do what he tells you." Joseph distributed crops from the storehouses, selling it to the world, but giving it to his brothers. He was accountable with his gift and to his God.

As a wealth harvester, you have the innate ability to access strategies from heaven. You have the enlarged capacity needed to hold the wealth of the nations. You have the ability to function as a walking storehouse for God's people. The wealth of the wicked is laid up for you to gather and distribute in His kingdom. The world around us needs what God has given and we are responsible for what He has imparted (see Deuteronomy 29:29).

> *Now do not be distressed or angry with yourselves because you sold me here, for God sent me ahead of you to save life and preserve our family. For the famine has been in the land these two years, and there are still five more years in which there will be no plowing and harvesting. God sent me [to Egypt] ahead of you to preserve for you a remnant on the earth, and to keep you alive by a great escape. I will provide for you and sustain you, so that you and your household and all that are yours may not become impoverished, for there are still five years of famine to come.*

> *Genesis 45:5-8, 11*

What a powerful display of humility and selflessness! Joseph further told his brothers, "What the enemy meant evil, God meant it for good"(see Genesis 50:20). At that moment, Joseph understood his purpose. He could articulate why he had to endure everything he'd gone through. He realized that he was not only responsible for his own belly, but for the bellies of his family and the nation. He knew that the impoverishment his soul suffered in the pit produced the power to hold wealth for a greater good. His temporarily stripped life produced a wealth of experience that fed the impoverished. He realized the gift in him matched a need outside of him. He knew he couldn't afford to operate in resentment and offense because he'd already paid such a huge price.

Breaking ground is unearthing, and it commands a strength that many cannot fathom. It requires maturity. It requires foresight. It requires humility. It requires boldness and authority that can only be found in the pit. The pain inflicted upon me by others was not about them. It was about what God needed to process out of *me*. I was afraid of men in their faces; their opinions. There was deliverance available, but the deliverance was in the pit. And when it was time to come out, I emerged stronger. I'm healed; I know who I am. I'm no longer afraid. I'm not angry or embittered. I cannot allow anger to grow roots in my heart. My giving will not be based upon reciprocity but generosity. I also realize that the attack didn't originate with them, there was a spirit of jealousy trying to terminate my destiny.

YOU CAN'T FEED THE NATIONS IF YOU'RE
SPIRITUALLY IMPOVERISHED.

You don't have time to focus on who hurt you. Get healed today. You have kingdom business to take care of. You cannot devote time to insignificant earthly squabbles. "Yes, feast your mind on all the treasures of the heavenly realm and fill your thoughts with heavenly realities, and not with the distractions of the natural realm" (Colossians 3:2, TPT). Don't focus on the hate or envy. Instead, ask God why He's allowing it, so you can move forward in your purpose in love. What blueprint has God placed in your hands? Time is of the essence because as I look around, I see famine in the land; a deluge of poverty is attempting to overwhelm God's people. It breaks my heart to witness the level of lack in this world.

The term "potter's field," originates in Matthew 27:3-8. After Judas betrayed Jesus, he was so full of guilt and regret that he returned the 30 pieces of silver he was paid for his role in the betrayal. The chief priests and elders wouldn't put the money back into the treasury as it was considered "blood money." Instead, they used it to purchase a potter's field also called the "Field of Blood." This field was used to bury the poor, foreigners, those who committed suicide, and others who were considered "unfit" for a traditional Jewish burial. Let's read what God says about that.

> *But the stranger who resides with you shall be to you like someone native-born among you; and you shall love him as yourself, for you were strangers in the land of Egypt; I am the Lord your God.*
>
> *Leviticus 19:34*

> *Speak up for those who cannot speak for themselves, for the rights of all who are destitute. Speak up and judge fairly; defend the rights of the poor and needy.*
>
> *Proverbs 31:8-9*

The Scriptures above are only two of many where God demands that the poor and foreigners be treated with dignity and respect, yet religious leaders decided to take the very blood money from Jesus' betrayal and once again betray Him by disobeying Him.

> *So when they had finished breakfast, Jesus said to Simon Peter, "Simon, son of John, do you love*

Me more than these [others do—with total commitment and devotion]?" He said to Him, "Yes, Lord; You know that I love You [with a deep, personal affection, as for a close friend]." Jesus said to him, "Feed My lambs."

John 21:15

Sermons are great, teachings are excellent, and church attendance is vital, but we must feed the sheep of God as well. Sometimes people can't hear the Word God has given you, above the rumbling of their bellies. Sometimes people won't serve a Jesus they can't see in you. Have we created our own spiritual potter's field by neglecting the needs that are so evident around us? Are we guilty of betraying Jesus by burying His sheep hungry? Are we watching people starve on earth physically and spiritually, die empty and go to hell? Is exegesis all we have to offer? It's time to close our mouths long enough to open our wallets. We will see the kingdom of heaven advance even further when bellies are full of the Gospel, but also full of bread. We are spiritual beings housed by physical bodies; they both must be fed (see James 2:15-16).

The grace of God does not end with preaching a sermon, interpreting a dream, or giving a prophecy. We have kingdoms to overthrow. We have infrastructures of wealth to build. We have nations to shift. At some point, our spiritual gifts must produce something tangible in the earth. Trust God to release His varied wisdom in your life today. Decide today to die empty of the manifold grace in you so that the world around you dies full. Let's stop attempting to put a boundaryless God in religious boxes of humanistic design. There are enough selfish unholy buildings of babel in world systems as it is.

Exodus 1: 8, 11 reads:

Then a new king, to whom Joseph meant nothing, came to power in Egypt. "Look," he said to his people, "the Israelites have become far too numerous for us. So, they put slave masters over them to oppress them with forced labor, and they built Pithom and Rameses as store cities for Pharaoh.

The new Pharaoh disregarded Joseph but used his blueprint for harvesting wealth. It is said that the ruins of the store cities, *Pithom and Ramses* were found as recently as 1883. Evidence reveals that they were partly built with bricks without straw. Under the whip of Pharaoh, the Israelites were forced to build those cities and without the necessary resources. This was an unreasonable and heartless form of punishment as the straw served as a binder to keep the bricks from crumbling. Not only were they enslaved to build for the enemy but also supply the resources themselves (see Exodus 5:7). Pithom and Rameses were used to store agricultural provisions, military supplies, and weapons. So, under the demand of evil tyrants, God's people made room for the very weapons to be used against them.

The counterfeiter of this world—Satan—attempts to imitate and use God's principles for unwholesome purposes. The world spheres in which we live are founded upon unethical practices that mock God. However, no longer will God's wealth harvesters build upon a foundation faulty from the start. God is releasing His people to build from the ground up structures of abundance. It will all come by something the enemy cannot duplicate… the manifold wisdom of God.

In closing, I want to say that there is a need in the earth crying out for the harvest in you. So God is about to release His servants from their pits and dungeons in a hurry with unlimited resources. And to the world, it would appear you are some overnight success. However, there are no overnight successes in the kingdom, only underground pit prodigies trained intensively by the Lord of the Harvest.

5

THE SOLOMONIC MODEL

KINGDOM WEALTH HARVESTERS ARE designed to carry the weighty, choice things of God. They have the incredible responsibility of dispensing kingly resources for kingly assignments. And as the richest king to have ever lived, I can think of no better person to introduce in this chapter than King Solomon. Worth an estimated 2.2 trillion dollars by today's standard, Scripture reveals that King Solomon brought in 40 billion dollars in gold as a tribute in trading alone. As an international trader, he grossed millions in a single month from multiple streams of income. To hold his great riches Solomon practiced store housing. He built cities, towns, and supply centers of immeasurable wealth and supplies. Whatever there was to be owned he owned it. Whatever there was to be purchased he could afford it. Whatever indulgent delicacy there was to partake of, to it, he had access. He says it best in his own words. "Whatever my eyes looked at with desire I did not refuse them. I did not withhold from my heart any pleasure" (Ecclesiastes 2:10a).

> *And he will be like a tree firmly planted [and fed]*
> *by streams of water, Which yields its fruit in its*
> *season; Its leaf does not wither; And in whatever*
> *he does, he prospers [and comes to maturity].*
>
> *Psalm 1:3*

As a wealth harvester, God will flow multiple streams of income to you. You will gross a seemingly endless amount of resources, but you must be planted firmly in Him, so it doesn't drown you. There are certain characteristics required to function successfully in this degree of wealth. We will discuss three of them below.

OPERATE IN GODLY WISDOM

Solomon was wealthy beyond belief but his trillionaire status didn't start with a great idea from his imagination. It didn't begin with a great team of business associates. Neither did it commence with a course on becoming wealthy. Though already an heir, Solomon's wisdom for multiplication of wealth originated with an impartation from a dream. In this dream, God appeared to him and offered him anything his heart so desired. Read Solomon's desire below.

> *So now, O Lord my God, You have made Your*
> *servant king in place of David my father; and as*

for me, I am but a little boy [in wisdom and experience]; I do not know how to go out or come in [that is, how to conduct business as a king].

1 Kings 3:7

Even though Solomon had a lack of wisdom in kingship, he was wise enough to petition the Source of Wisdom. He understood that it was better to get wisdom than gold and to choose understanding than silver (see Proverbs 16:16). Solomon understood that he needed God for successful business acumen.

For wisdom is a protection even as money is a protection, but the [excellent] advantage of knowledge is that wisdom shields and preserves the lives of its possessors.

Ecclesiastes 7:12

It's vitally important for those who are called wealth harvesters to have Godly wisdom. Because while some trust in their wealth, in the end, it will prove as an unfaithful protector. The wisdom of God shields and preserves the lives of those submitted to it. It adds longevity, gives insight and multiplicity. It all boils down to one question… who do you really trust as your protector and defense?

Consider the person who guesses seven "lucky" numbers and wins millions in the lottery. That individual becomes an instant millionaire on the outside, but often inside he's still poor. The wealth outside of him has no space inside of him. Simply put, his mindset doesn't match his new reality. And all too often just as quickly as the windfall of wealth is received, it is lost. "Wealth from get-rich-schemes quickly disappears" (Proverbs 13:11a). When you find an individual that lacks wisdom, they often lack the ability to sustain wealth because there's no capacity to hold it. You will also find that they lack the ability to access wealth again because wisdom wasn't imparted from a worthy Source.

MONEY CAN TAKE YOU PLACES WHERE ONLY
WISDOM CAN PLANT YOU.

However, the person whose ark has been prepared can navigate torrents of wealth. A prepared vessel built strong in wisdom could lose everything and then build it again overnight. How? It's being constructed from an inside resource of greater wisdom (see 1 John 4:4). Because we have the Risen Savior living on the inside of us, we have resurrection power in us. We have the power to speak to dead things and call them to life. Because we have the Divine Creator imparting us with wisdom, we can produce something out of nothing. That power has the potential to multiply, regenerate, and replenish the earth (see Genesis 1:28).

> *If any of you lacks wisdom [to guide him through a decision or circumstance] he is to ask of [our benevolent] God, who gives to everyone generously and without rebuke or blame, and it will be given to him.*
>
> *James 1:5*

God will always require us to achieve something that's beyond our limitations. It will be so great that you can only accomplish it by asking for His wisdom. If you haven't done so, pause and ask God to give you the wisdom needed for your business, ministry, or relationship. Admit to Him that you're lost without Him. You'll find that God is not like humans. He's liberal with His wisdom and generous with His knowledge. He knows how high His plans are and He knows that our finite minds can't reach them on our own. It pleases God when we put Him first, acknowledging Him as our Guide.

> *Now it pleased the Lord that Solomon had asked this thing. God said to him, because you have asked this and have not asked for yourself a long life nor for wealth, nor for the lives of your enemies, but have asked for yourself understanding to recognize justice.*
>
> *1 Kings 3:10-11*

Because Solomon asked for wisdom, God superseded his request going above and beyond, giving him unheard of wisdom accompanied by unheard of wealth.

WISDOM ATTRACTS WEALTH.

Remember that "wisdom is the most important thing" (see Proverbs 4:7a). Without it, anything gained has the potential to be nothing more than "filthy lucre," built upon worldly values. Even "if it costs everything you have to get understanding. Treasure wisdom and it will make you great hold on to it and it will bring you honor" (Proverbs 4:7b-9). Solomon's name was made great, and he received immense honor based upon wisdom. Kings and queens were attracted to him.

> *When the queen of Sheba had seen all the wisdom of Solomon, and the house (palace) which he had built, the food on his table, the seating of his servants (court officials), the attendance of his waiters and their attire, his cupbearers,*

*his stairway by which he went up to the
house(temple) of the Lord, she was breathless
and awed [by the wonder of it all].*

1 Kings 10:4-5

Queen Sheba was left "breathless." She couldn't fathom the excellency of King Solomon's reign. As queen, she must've known many great men during her time, however, she found none to be like Solomon. What set him apart?

*When she came to Solomon, she spoke with him
about everything that was on her mind [to
discover the extent of his wisdom]. Solomon
answered all her questions; there was nothing
hidden from the king which he did not explain to
her. Then she told the king, "The report which I
heard in my own land about your words and
wisdom is true! I did not believe the report until
I came and saw it with my own eyes.*

1 Kings 10:2b,6-7

The wisdom of God was so evident in the life of Solomon that even a woman who didn't know God was able to discern Him.

As God releases wisdom in your life, an overabundance of wealth will be attracted to it. You will attract kings, queens, and moguls of various world spheres. Wealth harvesters must be wealthy because they are called to bring glory to God's name not only in the four walls of the church building but in the four corners of the earth. What does wealth have to do with bringing glory to God's name in the world? There's a certain group of people who won't listen to you if they don't respect you. Sometimes respect isn't given unless results are "seen with their own eyes" (see Proverbs 13:22). This is proven in Ecclesiastes 9:14-16:

> *Once there was a small town with only a few people in it. One day, out of nowhere, a king and his powerful army marched against it, surrounded it, and besieged it. The villagers didn't know how to fend off such a powerful enemy. But one man, who was very poor but very wise, rallied the villagers and managed to drive the army away. So, I said, "Wisdom is better than strength." But the wisdom of the poor is despised; nobody listens to their wise counsel.*

While we must not use wealth to advance our kingdom, God can use them to advance His. Unfortunately, many refuse to see God unless they see evidence. Sheba set out to "test" Solomon's wisdom first, but then she focused solely on his materialistic possessions. While wisdom is an invaluable asset and a wealth in its own right, some despise it if there is no fruit of its existence. In some cases, wisdom alone is not enough. Ecclesiastes 7:11 says, "wisdom is better when it comes with money [an inheritance]."

> *Then she gave the king about nine thousand pounds [one hundred and twenty talents] of gold and many spices and jewels [precious stones]. No one since that time has brought more spices than the queen of Sheba gave to King Solomon. So, Solomon had more riches and wisdom than all the other kings on earth.*
>
> *1 Kings 10:10, EXB*

Impressed, Queen Sheba poured even more wealth into Solomon's kingdom. She gave gifts unsurpassed by any gift to have ever been given. Why? Because "the wealth of the wicked is laid up for the just." There is something greater than money that this rich, empty world needs; they need the wealth of the wisdom of God inside of you.

OPERATE IN KINGLY WEIGHT

When I first began weight training, I started out with very light weights. However, with consistent training, I've increased in overall muscle tone and weight. Over time, I've noticed that the more muscle I developed, the stronger I became. The stronger I became, the more weight I was able to lift. I am now able to leg press 400 pounds when at one point 50 pounds felt like a ton of bricks. When lifting weights, you are actually tearing and damaging your muscles. This is the reason muscle soreness is often experienced days following. However, once your muscles have rested and healed, they become larger with the ability to handle more weight.

Some of you are feeling torn down and you're wondering whether you're on the correct path. The answer is yes. God is simply conditioning you to handle more. He cannot put tomorrow's weight of destiny on today's level of endurance. All too often, some are prematurely placed upon stages based on talent, skill, and earthly favor alone. As said earlier, if a platform outweighs your character, it will crush you. Thus, the enemies you're fighting today are from your tomorrow. Resistance brings strength and every trial and difficulty you have stood up under only made your legs strong enough to carry the weight of your assignment.

> *For our momentary, light distress [this passing trouble] is producing for us an eternal weight of glory [a fullness] beyond all measure [surpassing*

all comparisons, a transcendent splendor, and an endless blessedness].

2 Corinthians 4:17

The word "light" used above is from the Hebrew word *elapronos* which means "lightweight, easy, or simple." The trials we carry feel heavy, however, they're training you to handle the heavy weight of glory being produced in your life. The weight of glory is something that everyone wants but nobody wants. Meaning everyone wants the weight of glory, but nobody wants the weight of pressure that comes along with it. There is an eternal weight of glory that God wishes to release upon you, but if you can't handle the light weight of trials, you can't handle the weight of wealth. If you can't run with the footmen on your current level, how will you contend with the horseman on the next level (see Jeremiah 12:5).

When you were on the verge of suicide but trusted God instead, your weight increased. When everyone turned their backs on you, but you held on to God, your weight increased. When people hurt you, but you allowed God to heal your heart, your weight increased. And if you look back over your life, you'll find the problems that once seemed weighty are now lightweight issues unworthy of your time and the exertion of your energy. You are stronger and weightier than you've ever been. Though the weight is unseen to the natural eye, it is respected where it's relevant; it is acknowledged in the spiritual realm where the fight for your destiny ensues. The heavy weight of your trials served as God's training mechanisms to increase your weight to compliment the weight of your destiny.

First Chronicles 20 depicts the story of one of David's many conquests. While gathering the spoil of conquered territory, he discovered the crown of another king.

David took the crown from their king from his head and found that it weighed a talent of gold and that there was precious stone in it; so, it was set on David's head.

1 Chronicles 20:2

In Biblical times, the value of money depended on its weight. The heavier the coin the greater the value. The Scripture above is remarkable because a talent of gold weighs nearly 130 pounds, yet David had the ability to wear it on his head. This puzzled me. How were both kings able to withstand the load of this weighty crown? It was because their kingly weight matched the weight of the crown.

"HEAVY IS THE HEAD THAT WEARS THE CROWN."

KING VI

In Deuteronomy 8:18 it is written that God gives us the power to get wealth. The word "power" as used there comes from the Hebrew word *koach*. Koach is translated as "human strength, capacity, produce, and wealth of soil." The wealth harvester must be made strong because the wealth of the soil is heavy. Wealth is weight and you must have broad shoulders and a strong back to carry all the issues it embodies. With wealth comes a diverse set of difficulties. With it often comes influence, fame, leeches, and enemies. You must be tough to stand underneath the pressures it brings. Heavy is the burden of a wealth harvester. Weighty is the call of a kingdom financier.

OPERATE IN SELFLESSNESS

Solomon could've asked God for anything in the world, but he selflessly asked for wisdom to conduct business in the kingdom. He put the work that God entrusted to him to the forefront of his heart. Likewise, wealth harvesters called according to the Solomonic Model are called to be selfless individuals. God cannot release wealth into the hands of selfish people only interested in their own agendas.

When my finances were in ruin, I wondered why God wasn't changing my situation. One day I went down a list of things that I *was* and I *wasn't* to God. I finally screamed, "I'm not selfish, I give to people." God said that it was not about my ability to be "unselfish," but my inability to be selfless.

Often times, the words unselfish and selfless are used interchangeably. However, while the words are similar, they are different. Unselfish is simply defined as "not selfish, generous, or altruistic." Selflessness is on a whole other level. It means "having little or no concern for oneself," especially with regard to fame, position, money, or acknowledgment. Apostle Paul echoes this sentiment below.

> *[But] I don't care about my own life [consider my life worth anything]. The most important thing [or My only goal] is that I complete [finish] my mission [task; course; race; the work [ministry; service] that the Lord Jesus gave me [I received from the Lord Jesus]—to tell people [testify/witness to] the Good News [Gospel] about God's grace.*
>
> *Acts 20:24*

As I thought about what God had spoken, my mind went back to an incident that happened earlier that day at the gym. As I sat on an abdominal machine, I witnessed a staggering woman tumbling until she finally hit the ground. My immediate response was to help. However, in my heart, I couldn't help but think about how great I was to help her when others around didn't notice or seem to care. Sadly, I secretly vied for accolades. I was unselfish in my act, but I wasn't selfless in my heart. A selfless person gives of himself even when it costs him something and without recompense.

This dying and fallen world needs individuals without ulterior motives. They need trustworthy people who operate in the love of Jesus, expecting nothing in return. This world needs people likened to the Apostle Paul who counted himself as nothing, but the ministry given by God as everything. You must "abandon every display of selfishness. Possess a greater concern for what matters to others instead of your own interests" (Philippians 2:4). Second Corinthians 8:9 says:

> *For you are recognizing [more clearly] the grace of our Lord Jesus Christ [His astonishing kindness, His generosity, His gracious favor], that though He was rich, yet for your sake He became poor, so that by His poverty you might become rich (abundantly blessed).*

We serve the selfless Savior, Who, motivated by love came in human form to redeem us, to heal us; to give us life. He stepped out of heaven to step onto the earth to enrich us with His Presence. Even while we were yet sinners, Jesus didn't think twice about saving us. He suffered an agonizing death but considered what was "laid before Him" greater than what He was experiencing. Upon His shoulders was the weight of the sins of everyone. Jesus bench-pressed the entire world. Yet, He still gives us a choice whether we serve Him or not. He died, demanding nothing in return and if we are to be imitators of Christ, we are expected to imitate His selfless nature.

> *King Solomon also built cities for storing grain and supplies [supply centers/ cities/ towns] and cities for [towns to station] his chariots and horses. He built whatever he wanted in Jerusalem, Lebanon, and everywhere he ruled.*
>
> *1 Kings 9:19*

As Solomon was an expert in bringing in wealth to fund his kingdom, wealth harvesters are arising to bring in riches to advance God's kingdom. We will witness those with a kingly anointing operating in the wisdom of God, kingly weight, and selflessness harvest wealth as never before. God will provide extravagantly for His initiatives in this earth. A clear and undeniable trail of wealth will be laid along the path of those armed with His vision and His heart.

6

KINGLY PITFALLS

W E'VE DISCUSSED SOLOMON'S ACCOMPLISHMENTS at length. However, it is important to remember that even though he was successful and wealthy beyond belief and even though kings and queens sought him from all over the earth, his life still ended in tragedy. King Solomon's life paints a sad portrait of one being lifted into the heights of God, only to be lowered into the depths of sin. Solomon's life proves true that the higher the platform God places one on, the more disgraceful and visible one's fall has the potential to be. We first read of God's anger toward Solomon's betrayal in 1 Kings 11:9.

The Lord became angry with Solomon because his heart was turned away from the Lord, the God of Israel, who had appeared to him twice.

How could one who once pleased God, anger and disappoint Him? How could one who was so favored and blessed take such a disgraceful plunge? How could one who once valued the wisdom of God above everything else in the world abandon it for the world? For our benefit, it is necessary not only to explore Solomon's successes but also his failures. Thus, this chapter is devoted to five common pitfalls those who are called to wealth are susceptible to.

ENTITLEMENT

David's position as king solidified Solomon's position as his successor. Solomon was born into inherited wealth as King David earned millions in spoils from warfare alone. Generational blessings were upon his life. However, along with inherited blessings from King David came inherited sin.

Known as the man after God's own heart, David was one of great faith and affection for the Lord (see 1 Samuel 13:14). However, while David loved God, he exhibited great flaws. David was a millionaire, a warrior, an anointed musician, and a king. David was also a cheater, a fornicator, a liar, and a murderer. He was known as a man who once pursued his flesh as much as he pursued God. And most of his behavior stemmed from a sense of entitlement.

On one end, *entitlement* means "a right to benefits specified by law or contract" on the other it means "belief that one is deserving of certain privileges." So it is quite possible to be entitled to something but also exhibit an arrogant sense of entitlement.

After the death of Samuel, David moved into the Desert of Paran. It was there that Nabal, a wealthy fool (the meaning of his name) lived. Needing rations for himself and his men, David sent representatives to proposition Nabal for sustenance. His request was within reason as David had aided Nabal before by protecting his men in the desert. However, because David had not yet become world-renowned, Nabal responded disrespectfully and offered him no supplies. David became fiercely angry by the snub. Read below how he responds.

> David said to his men, "Each man put on your sword." So, each man put on his sword. David also put on his sword, and about four hundred men went up behind David while two hundred stayed back with the provisions and supplies.
>
> 1 Samuel 25:13

Though entitled to kingship, David's sense of entitlement arrogantly led him to believe that he was also deserving of Nabal's wealth. The same man who constantly sought the Lord's guidance did not in this case. Instead, David was ready to slay Nabal and his entire camp for wealth that didn't belong to him. The reality was that even though Nabal was a fool and would sovereignly meet his demise by the hand of God, David had no right to take matters into his own hands.

In my desert place, I battled feelings of entitlement. Because I'd helped, prayed for, and counseled many others before, I automatically expected my kindness to be reciprocated during the driest season of my life. But God isolated me; He stripped me from every voice I depended on. No one could help me even if they tried. I had to look to God as my Deliverer. In the desert place, I learned that no one owed me anything. I learned that my giving wasn't to be based on who could give back. It was to be an act of love.

We further witness David's brazen sense of entitlement on display in 2 Samuel 11:2-4a. It says:

> *One evening David got up from his couch and was walking on the [flat] roof of the king's palace, and from there he saw a woman bathing; and she was very beautiful in appearance. David sent word and inquired about the woman. Someone said, "Is this Bathsheba, the daughter of Eliam, the wife of Uriah the Hittite?" David sent messengers and took her.*

Embroiled by lust and entitlement, David went as far as to take and lie with another man's wife. This tawdry affair led to Bathsheba's pregnancy. However, instead of repenting and turning away from his sin, David devised a wicked scheme, abused his power, and murdered Uriah, *Bathsheba's husband*. It's interesting that even in the genealogy written in Matthew 1 Bathsheba is still referred to as the one that "had been the wife of Uriah." Because even though David was close to God's heart, his reprehensible actions would not just disappear. Not only did the illegitimate child that was conceived in sin die, but David's actions would have lingering effects on the lives of his other children.

> *Now, therefore, the sword shall never depart from your house, because you have despised Me and have taken the wife of Uriah the Hittite to be your wife. Thus, says the Lord, 'Behold, I will stir up evil against you from your own household.*
>
> *2 Samuel 12:10-11a*

Like an unrelenting infectious disease, murderous plots spread throughout David's family. His sin led to a revolt within his household. From that point, his children would rise against each other. Amon felt entitled to Tamar, his sister, so he raped her. Absalom felt entitled to justice for Tamar, so he killed Amon. Absalom felt entitled to his father's throne, so he attempted to overthrow David. Absalom's rebellion led to his death at the hand of Joab. Adonijah, David's son felt entitled to Solomon's throne, so Solomon ordered the deaths of both Adonijah and Joab. Like father like son, Solomon took the baton of entitlement and fell into many pitfalls.

1. THE PITFALL OF WEALTH HOARDING

Every man brought a gift [of tribute]: articles of silver and gold, garments, weapons, spices, horses, and mules, so much year by year. The king made silver as common in Jerusalem as stones, and cedars as plentiful as the sycamore trees that are in the lowland.

1 Kings 10:25, 27

Year by year, Solomon continued to increase in wealth, fame, and influence. He multiplied, and he grew. At face value, one could assume that the Lord was pleased with his actions. However, not all growth is good growth and not all increase is pleasing in the eyes of God. The truth was that while Solomon was increasing materially; he was decreasing spiritually. His connections with men and wealth were rising, but his relationship with God was declining. But exactly what was Solomon's great sin? Deuteronomy 17:17b commands, "the king must not have too much silver and gold." Because Solomon was already a trillionaire, one may wonder why a few

THE FOUNDATION of WEALTH

more trinkets of silver and gold would matter. It's because the issue wasn't the accrual of more possessions; The problem was Solomon's newfound inherited heart disease. His outward behavior of hoarding reflected his inward state. There was an accumulation of greed inside Solomon's heart. His obsession with gathering silver and gold equaled disobedience and rebellion. As a result, his God-given wealth distorted into filthy lucre—money obtained dishonestly.

The allure of money can become so strong that some continue to accumulate it at the expense of disobeying God. Luke 12 tells the parable of a wealthy, foolish farmer whose land was "fertile and productive." In fact, it was so fertile that it produced crops that exceeded his storage space. Instead of appreciating what was before him, he became obsessed with building and hoarding more. As a result, he tore down his storehouses to build larger ones to hold more crops. The disillusioned farmer said to himself, "I have stored enough for years. Now I can rest, eat, and be merry." Little did he know his soul would be required of him that very night. "So it is for the one who continues to store up and hoard possessions for himself and is not rich in his relationship with God" (Luke 12:21). Nothing that the busy farmer accumulated on earth would benefit him after his death. Thus, all of his efforts of building were done so in vain. His earthly harvest couldn't save his soul. What does it profit us to gain this whole world then lose our souls? (Matthew 16:26). The answer is nothing. There is nothing on the earth more valuable than our souls and spending eternity with Jesus.

> Some people store up treasures in their homes here on earth. This is a shortsighted practice—don't undertake it. Moths and rust will eat up any treasure you may store here. Thieves

may break into your homes and steal your
precious trinkets. Instead, put up your treasures
in heaven where moths do not attack, where rust
does not corrode, and where thieves are barred
at the door. For where your treasure is, there
your heart will be also.

Matthew 6:19-21

No matter how much wealth you've accumulated on this earth, if you've acquired it in a manner that is in outright disregard of God's commands, you're poor. You are a spiritually impoverished soul collecting meaningless knick-knacks on earth and nothing in heaven. This selfish ambition leads to an ever-perishing life, devoid of heavenly understanding. My prayer is that short-sightedness—what's right before you—isn't your portion in life. I pray God can trust you with His heavenly vision for your earthly harvest.

2. THE PITFALL OF DIVERTED TRUST

Solomon's horses were imported from Egypt and
from Kue, and the king's merchants acquired them
from Kue, for a price. A chariot could be imported
from Egypt for six hundred shekels of silver, and a
horse for a hundred and fifty; and in the same way
they exported them, by the king's merchants, to all
the kings of the Hittites and to the kings of Aram
(Syria).

1 Kings 10:28-29

Solomon persisted in his rebellion toward God. It is written in Deuteronomy 17:16 and again in Isaiah 31:1,3 that a "king must not have too many [multiply] horses for himself, and he must not send people to Egypt to get more horses." But again, the issue wasn't so much in the number of horses Solomon owned as it was where his trust was placed. By accumulating horses and chariots, he was accumulating security and safety. In essence, Solomon began placing his trust in armies and not in God. Psalm 20:7 says:

Some trust in chariots and some in horses, but we trust in the name of the LORD our God.

We cannot place our trust in human beings, connections, or material possessions. Because whatever you put your trust in, you worship. And whatever you worship, you serve. Trusting in and relying on anything besides God equals a path lined with deterioration.

3. THE PITFALL OF IDOLATRY

For when Solomon was old, his wives turned his heart away after other gods; and his heart was not completely devoted to the Lord his God, as was the heart of his father David.

1 Kings 11:4

Wealth, power, and influence were commonplace for King Solomon. He'd fallen into diverted trust. He'd succumb to wealth hoarding. Each sin possibly became easier and easier to commit. As a result, he continued to slip deeper in error. Solomon, in direct defiance to God's instruction, decided to "love" over one thousand "strange women." In doing so, he yoked himself with women who were yoked to other gods. God explicitly warns against idolatry because once something replaces God inside our hearts, obeying His voice is almost impossible.

1 Kings 11:5-7 says:

> *For Solomon went after Ashtoreth, the [fertility]*
> *goddess of the Sidonians, and after Milcom the*
> *horror (detestable idol) of the Ammonites.*
> *Solomon did evil [things] in the sight of the Lord,*
> *and did not follow the Lord fully, as his father*
> *David had done. Then Solomon built a high place*
> *for [worshiping] Chemosh the horror (detestable*
> *idol) of Moab, on the hill which is east of*
> *Jerusalem, and for Molech the horror (detestable*
> *idol) of the sons of Ammon.*

Solomon went after Ashtoreth, the goddess known for its "productive power and fertility." What's amazing is that in all God had produced and multiplied in his life, Solomon still sought power to produce fruit elsewhere. He was no longer a harvester for God's kingdom, but for the enemy. And the fruit Solomon produced would be deadly because everyone "that does not bear good fruit is cut down and thrown into the fire" (see Matthew 7:19).

One of the Hebrew words for idol is [14]*aven*, which means "nothingness." When Solomon opened his heart up to a false god of productivity, it left a void inside of him; "nothingness" filled him. He would find that the void could only be filled by God; a soul separated from God is a plagued empty soul. After Solomon could not fill his void with unproductive works, he looked to replace the King with a proxy. Solomon also worshipped Milcom which means "great king." Again, this led to nothingness as there is only one true and living God. He cannot be substituted. Solomon then built an altar to Chemosh, whose name means "subdue and destroyer." He became so subdued and encultured by the gods of his wives and concubines, that he lost sight of God's instruction. Sadly, Solomon would find that once he ceased building for God's kingdom that he built upon something that would end in his destruction. The works of his own hands would destroy him.

Wealth harvesters must remember that all true and good productive power comes from the Lord. Contrary to widespread belief, not all success is true success. In the book of Joshua, God promises "good success," so if there is good success then there must also be evil success. Anything produced by unholy methods ends in destruction. Remember the True King we serve and besides Him, there is no other. No trinket can ever take His place. With God and without a dime, we have everything. Without Him, with billions in the bank, we have nothingness.

> *...Solomon because up have done this and have not kept My covenants and My statutes, which I have commanded you, I will certainly tear the kingdom away from you and give it to your servant.*

> *1 Kings 11:11*

Solomon paid hefty repercussions for his abominations. The very kingdom he killed for, God stripped and gave to another. Make your allegiance sure! If you choose incorrectly, it will be the costliest decision you've ever made because you will pay with your soul. Listen and reflect upon the words of one who learned from experience, King Solomon, the wisest earthly king to have ever lived. Ecclesiastes 2:9,11 says:

> *So, I became great and excelled more than all who preceded me in Jerusalem. My wisdom also remained with me. Then I considered all which my hands had done and labored to do, and behold, all was vanity and chasing after the wind and there was no profit (nothing of lasting value) under the sun.*

OTHER KINGLY SUCCESSES AND PITFALLS

JEHOSHAPHAT

... All Judah brought tribute to Jehoshaphat, and he had great wealth and honor. His heart was encouraged, and he took great pride in the ways of the Lord; moreover, he again removed the high places [of pagan worship] and the Asherim from Judah. Some of the Philistines brought gifts and silver as tribute to Jehoshaphat; the Arabians also brought him flocks: 7,700 rams and 7,700 male goats. So, Jehoshaphat became greater and greater.

2 Chronicles 17:5-6, 11-12

The notoriety and wealth experienced by Jehoshaphat had not been seen in anyone since the days of King Solomon. And as in the case with Solomon, there is a visible pattern of the wisdom and favor of God attracting the wealth of the world. As they brought to him, he became "greater and greater." As his wealth increased, his favor increased. He served the Lord with extraordinary pride.

He built fortresses and storage cities in Judah. He had large supplies in the cities of Judah, and soldiers, courageous men, in Jerusalem.

2 Chronicles 17:13

While Solomon used store cities to secure provisions for himself and his kingdom, Jehoshaphat built store cities and fortresses to house weapons for soldiers. His storehouses held a wealth of weapons. God speaks of His own storehouse of weaponry in the Book of Job. It says:

Have you entered the storehouses of the snow, or have you seen the storehouses of the hail, which I have reserved for the time of trouble, for the day of battle and war?

Job 38:22

Deuteronomy 28:12 also speaks of God opening His good storehouse, the heavens, to give rain in its season. Deuteronomy 32 says that God has sealed up treasuries to be released at His will. This is good news. There is trouble in the land, in the form of poverty, but there is wealth stored up for God's harvesters to wield as weapons. In their possession, ordinary money becomes tools of mass destruction to combat wickedness in the earth. Deuteronomy 8:18 reads:

But you shall [earnestly] remember the Lord your God, for it is He Who gives you power to get wealth that He may establish His covenant which He swore to your fathers, as it is this day.

Wealth, as used above, is from the Hebrew word *chayil. Chayil,* mentioned over 200 times in Scripture, interprets as "strength, might, efficiency, army, and force." Thus, true wealth encompasses a multitude of blessings from the Lord. It includes strength, the ability to withstand times of trouble, the might, and the power to execute justice in the lives of the poor and needy. It includes efficiency to be effective at whatever we put our hands to. True wealth is a force from God against the forces of evil. Wealth harvesting is not merely about writing checks. It requires much more than that. Jehoshaphat built "strong fortresses." A fortress is something that protects. Wealth from God protects and defends as an army protects its country (see Ecclesiastes 7:12). Therefore, the enemy cannot come into our camp and steal what God has given. Wealth harvesters are kingdom protectors. With wealth, we cover needs. With wealth, we cover assignments. We protect what is precious in the eyes of God. And because we produce for Him, our wealth is protected by Him.

> *Beat your plowshares into swords and your pruning hooks into spears; Let the weak say, I am strong. Let the nations be stirred [to action] And come up to the Valley of Jehoshaphat, For there I will sit to judge and punish all the surrounding nations. Put in the sickle [of judgment], for the harvest is ripe; Come, tread [the grapes], for the wine press is full; The vats overflow, for the wickedness [of the people] is great.*
>
> *Joel 3:10, 12-13*

The weapon of wealth in your hand will take down principalities, destroy systems, and bring souls into the kingdom in mass proportions. Territory will be conquered for the Lord's purposes. You will take cities and monopolize enterprises by supplying the troops on the front line of ministry with provisions.

WEALTH HARVESTERS TAKE NATIONS FOR THE
KINGDOM.

It is written that Jehoshaphat had a passion to destroy the "high places" of the enemy. Likewise, those who God calls wealth harvesters are passionate about seeing the kingdom of Heaven erected and everything unlike it destroyed. In the hand of a wealth harvester, money is a missile and its target is every high thing that exalts itself against the knowledge of Christ (see 2 Corinthians 10:5).

THE FOUNDATION of WEALTH

Again, it is important to mention that while Jehoshaphat accomplished much in the name of the Lord, like Solomon, he fell into a pitfall.

4. THE PITFALL OF ILLEGAL ALLIANCES

> *After [all] this Jehoshaphat king of Judah made an alliance with Ahaziah king of Israel, and he acted wickedly in doing so. He joined him in building ships to go to Tarshish [for trade], and they built them in Ezion-geber. Then Eliezer the son of Dodavahu of Mareshah prophesied against Jehoshaphat, saying, "Because you have allied yourself with Ahaziah, the Lord has broken down what you have built." So, the ships were wrecked and were unable to go to Tarshish.*

> *2 Chronicles 20:35-37*

In the beginning one of the first tasks God accomplished was separating darkness from light and for good reason (see Genesis 1). Scripture commands us against being "unequally yoked with nonbelievers." The NLT translation says, "Don't team up with those who are unbelievers. How can righteousness be a partner with wickedness? How can light live with darkness?" (2 Corinthians 6:14). According to the *Adam Clarke Commentary*, "yoked" is a military term that simply means to keep your own ranks. The Scripture above is admonishing us to stay in our positions and not join alliances with heathens. It is commanding us to stay and fight on the winning team and not break rank joining in the abominations of this world. Why? Unbelievers can cause our hearts to stray away from the Truth. What we behold, we become.

Jehoshaphat went into business with Ahaziah, establishing an illegal alliance. So, the ocean of wealth God allowed

Jehoshaphat to navigate, he used to build, and sail ships on with the enemy.

So often, I see those whom God has elevated on highly visible stages join forces with the very ones they were called to convert. God entrusted that individual with influence in a sphere of society to affect it for the good. However, before long the Christian and the sinner are indistinguishable. While we are a part of the world and interact with unbelievers, we are not to become intimate with them to the point that we forget Who we serve. Jesus sat with debt collectors, harlots, and sinners but He was the change agent. Similarly, we may be called to sit in places with unbelievers, but we are called to transform the world not be transformed by the world. We must always be the change agent and not be changed by the agent. Once you're ingrained in the world, the world is ingrained in you; Beelzebub cannot cast out Beelzebub (see Matthew 12:27).

> *Cling to your faith in Christ and keep your conscience clear. For some people have deliberately violated their consciences; as a result, their faith has been shipwrecked.*
>
> *1 Timothy 1: 19*

Just as Jehoshaphat's plans were thwarted by a shipwreck so will all those who have allowed their faith to be tainted by the world. Shipwrecked faith equals a shipwrecked life.

HEZEKIAH

> *Now Hezekiah had immense wealth and honor; and he made for himself treasuries for silver, gold, precious stones, spices, shields, and all kinds of delightful articles, and storehouses for the produce of grain, new wine, and [olive] oil, and stalls for all kinds of cattle, and sheepfolds*

for the flocks. Moreover, he made cities for himself and acquired an abundance of flocks and herds, for God gave him very many possessions.

2 Chronicles 32: 27-29

As with Solomon, God increased Hezekiah immensely in wisdom and wealth. Like Jehoshaphat, he tore down high places of worship. In fact, he was so passionate about uprooting evil that he destroyed a snake god that had been worshipped for 900 years prior. He trusted in God and there was no king like him among Judah before or after him (see 2 Kings 18:5). However, his deep devotion made him a ready target for the enemy. Because of his passionate affection and building efforts for the Lord, threats poured in.

Hezekiah received the letter from the hand of the messengers and read it. Then he went up to the house (temple) of the Lord and spread it out before the Lord.

2 Kings 19:14

Sennacherib, an Assyrian king came up against all the cities of Judah—except Jerusalem—and seized them. He then proceeded to send letters to Hezekiah threatening to capture Jerusalem as well. He was sadly mistaken. It appears that Sennacherib discounted the wisdom Hezekiah received from God.

...Hezekiah also stopped up the upper outlet of the waters of Gihon and channeled them down to the west side of the City of David. Hezekiah succeeded in everything that he did.

2 Chronicles 32:30

Hezekiah was a master military strategist. He built a watercourse, the Siloam Tunnel, to prepare for an impending attack from the Assyrians. In doing so, he also stopped up the watercourse of Gohin. By blocking the waters, this forced the Assyrians to travel the path through the City of David. Any surprise attack from the Assyrians would only come as a surprise to them because Jerusalem would be prepared. They'd know exactly where to expect them.

A watercourse is a channel built for streams of water to flow. Wealth harvesters are strategists that build multiple streams of income and uses the wealth to block the enemy's advances in the earth. The enemy is forced into submission and thrown into confusion as a result of the strategy given by God.

> O Lord, bend down Your ear and hear; Lord, open Your eyes and see; hear the [taunting] words of Sennacherib, which he has sent to taunt and defy the living God.
>
> *2 Kings 19:16*

Not only an expert strategist, Hezekiah was also a man of prayer. He was unashamed to cry out to God for the wisdom needed to go forth in battle. In fact, quite often he encouraged his men while preparing for war. He reminded them that though the opposing force had a multitude of people against them that the One with them was greater than the one with the king of Assyria (see 2 Chronicles 32:7). Hezekiah was able to look past natural circumstances and rely on the supernatural power of his God.

Likewise, wealth harvesters are to be given to prayer and rely on the abilities of God. They should recognize that ultimately God has the power to deliver them from the hand of the enemy. They must trust in Him and not their immediate circumstances.

Because of Hezekiah's deepened trust, God promises him that Sennacherib would not seize Jerusalem. He also gives him a sign in 2 Kings 19: 29 which says:

> *Then this shall be the sign [of these things] to you [Hezekiah]: this year you will eat what grows of itself, in the second year what springs up voluntarily, and in the third-year sow and reap, plant vineyards, and eat their fruit.*

Not only would the Assyrian king fail miserably in taking hold of Jerusalem, but God promised a harvest for Hezekiah's faithfulness. Yet even in Hezekiah's wisdom, wealth, trust, and favor, he still fell short.

5. THE PITFALL OF PRIDE

> *But Hezekiah did nothing [for the Lord] in return for the benefit bestowed on him, because his heart had become proud; therefore, God's wrath came on him and on Judah and Jerusalem.*
>
> *2 Chronicles 32:25*

Similarly, as with Solomon, Hezekiah proceeds to disappoint God despite all He had done for him. A man who once trusted God and valued His voice became proud in his heart and forgot Him. Scripture reveals that the stronghold of pride resurfaces in Hezekiah's heart time and time again.

> *Hezekiah received the envoys and showed them all that was in his storehouses—the silver, the gold, the spices, and the fine olive oil—his armory and everything found among his*

treasures. There was nothing in his palace or in all his kingdom that Hezekiah did not show them.

2 Kings 20:12

Marduk-Baladan was a deceiving envoy sent by a Babylonian king to spy out Hezekiah's kingdom. Enamored by his own glory, Hezekiah forfeited common sense. Caught up in pride, he blindly allowed the enemy into his domain. Scripture reveals that Hezekiah was pleased to show the Babylonian representative *his* treasure and *his* entire armory. In fact, there was nothing in *his* house that he did not show. Little did he know, God was testing *his* heart and unfortunately, he failed. When God looked inside of Hezekiah, He found that the very possessions He'd given, took possession in his heart. He was filled with egotism.

And so in the matter of the envoys of the rulers of Babylon, who were sent to him to inquire about the wonder that had happened in the land, God left him alone only to test him, in order to know everything that was in his heart.

2 Chronicles 32:31

Hezekiah's eyes were blinded to the truth by the pride of life. And everything that he had stored up was stripped away because pride was stored up in his heart.

Then Isaiah said to Hezekiah, "Hear the word of the Lord of hosts, 'Listen carefully, the days are coming when everything that is in your house and everything that your predecessors have stored up until this day will be carried to Babylon; nothing will be left,' says the Lord.

2 Kings 20:16-17

Proverbs 16:18 says, "Pride leads to destruction [comes before a disaster]; a proud attitude brings ruin [pride comes before a fall]. Wealth harvesters are born to breed successes.

However, great success often makes one more vulnerable to great ruin. It is important to guard your heart, never allowing the enemy in that territory. When God blesses you as a harvester of wealth, there will be tests. With massive influence comes huge tests. When God examines your heart, may He find it free from the snares of this world.

7

UNFAITHFUL HUSBANDMEN

PLANTED IN A LUXURIOUS garden filled with the manifest Presence of God, Adam was the earth's very first husbandman. The Garden of Eden was no ordinary run- of-the-mill garden. Overflowing with beautiful trees and pure cascading streams, Eden was a land of wealth laced in pure gold, bdellium (pearls), and onyx (see Genesis 2:12). The word *Eden* translates in Hebrew as "delight" or "the land of happiness." Eden was an opulent place of pleasure, abundance, and glory. It was God's own Garden of Paradise, untainted by evil and the contamination of sin.

No shrub or plant of the field was yet in the earth, and no herb of the field had yet sprouted, for the Lord God had not caused it to rain on the earth, and there was no man to cultivate the ground.

Genesis 2:5

In Chapter 1, it's written that plants were created; in Chapter 2, it's stated they were not yet created. Some believe that Genesis 1:11 and Genesis 2:5 are direct contradictions of one another. However, the plants created in Genesis 1 are a different set from those in chapter 2. God created the first set of plants for beauty and splendor; He created the latter for survival. Genesis 1:11 refers to vegetation such as flowers, grass (*desch*), trees (*ets-pariy*), and seed yielding plants (*eber-mazria-zera*). Genesis 2:5 describes *eber-hassadeh*, the "shrubs of the field," and "plants of the field." The plants of the field were cultivated grains, farm plants, and crops that Adam would have the divine responsibility of overseeing for his own sustenance. Desiring to allow humankind to partake in His creation, God created Adam in Genesis 2:7. God didn't send rain or plant crops until it was time for the husbandman to get into position.

The Lord God [took and] put the man [or Adam] in the Garden of Eden to care for [or till] it and work [take care of; look after] it.

Genesis 2:15, EXB

Centered in the middle of paradise, God simply told Adam to "tend and watch over" the garden. What a wonderful responsibility bestowed upon him. Adam was to till and harvest crops in a Garden that was already tangibly sustained by the King of Creation Himself. This would mean that even though Adam was told to "till" he wouldn't have to toil. The Garden was a blessed place and the "blessing of the Lord make rich and adds no toil" (see Proverbs 10:22). Adam was to supervise and protect an already fruitful land.

> *The Lord God made all sorts of trees grow up from the ground—trees that were beautiful and that produced delicious fruit. In the middle of the garden he placed the tree of life and the tree of the knowledge of good and evil.*
>
> *Genesis 2:9, NLT*

Until this point, everything God created was "good." However, in His omniscience, God knew that it would be better. So after creating Adam whose name means "to make," God created Eve, whose name means "living." Alone Adam could "make," or "build" but it would take Eve to give birth to new living breathing beings on earth. Together, Adam and Eve had the authority to "make living" or to procreate in the earth. Created in the very image of God, they were not only farmers of the garden, but co-creators with the Creator. And God said that this was not only good but "very good."

Adam's duty as a husbandman came with only one warning written in Genesis 2:16-17. It is there where God instructed him not to eat fruit from the tree which gave the knowledge of good and evil. If he did, he would die. The enemy, knowing that it was Adam who received the commandment, targeted Eve, and approached her with a cunning proposition.

> *Now the serpent was more crafty (subtle, skilled in deceit) than any living creature of the field which the Lord God had made. And the serpent (Satan) said to the woman, "Can it really be that God has said, 'You shall not eat from any tree of the garden'?*
>
> *Genesis 3:1*

Crafty means "being skilled in creative activity." Because Adam and Eve were purposed to procreate with the Creator, the enemy presented himself as a crafty creator. "No wonder, because satan masquerades as an angel [messenger]of light [trying to fool people into thinking he is from God, who is pure light] (2 Corinthians 11:14).

> *And when the woman saw that the tree was good for food, and that it was delightful to look at, and a tree to be desired in order to make one wise and insightful, she took some of its fruit and ate it; and she also gave some to her husband with her, and he ate.*
>
> *Genesis 3:6*

Taking the bait of Satan, Eve was deceived. She was led astray by the lust of the eyes—the beauty of the fruit, the lust of her flesh—the taste of the fruit, and the pride of life—the desire to be as wise as God (see 1 John 2:16). Because the fruit appealed to the senses of her flesh, Eve began to trust in the fruit and not in the Creator of the fruit. Driven by a desire to be equivalent to God—just like the deceiver—Adam and Eve once partners with the Creator hid from Him like renegades. But God knew their address. Listen to the consequences of their actions written in Genesis 3:17b-19:

> *The ground is [now] under a curse because of you; In sorrow and toil you shall eat [the fruit] of it. All the days of your life. "Both thorns and thistles it shall grow for you; And you shall eat the plants of the field. By the sweat of your face You will eat bread until you return to the ground, for from it you were taken; For you are dust, and to dust you shall return."*

Unfaithful Husbandmen

The unadulterated rebellion of Adam and Eve caused banishment from their effortless Garden of Grandeur. They were demoted to positions of sweat and toil. Once eternal beings, clothed in the glory of God, they joined alliances with a counterfeit creator. As a result, they were clothed in humanity and death was introduced into the earth. Now subjected to death and dying things, the grounds that once produced a harvest of treasure, gold, and fruit would yield thorns and weeds.

> *[In that day] In every vineyard [place] where there were a thousand grapevines worth twenty-five pounds [a thousand pieces] of silver, there will be only weeds [briers] and thorns.*
>
> *Isaiah 7:23*

Wealth harvesters must rely on the providence of God. God's providence upholds existence and inside of it is our existence. This means that when God positions you in your good land, He will sustain it because He ordained it. A synonym for providence is *husbandry*. The land that God gives will be toil free when we rely on God's husbandry and not our flesh. This is important because if we're not careful, the very land of wealth, lucrativeness and grace will transform into a dry place of thorns, weeds, lack, and death. Though not all the time physical death—as suggested by the counterfeiter in the Garden—but spiritual suicide where the land of growth and prosperity will cause you to reap what you've sown in toil. We mustn't allow this world to lure us in and away from what God has clearly instructed us to do. Obedience is key. Our trust must always be in God and not the fruit of the land. Fleshly efforts always yield sweat and destruction, but when we flow in the grace of God, we will surely flow in His abundance.

CAIN

Adam had sexual relations with [knew] his wife Eve, and she because pregnant [conceived] and gave birth to Cain. "With the Lord's help I have given birth to [produced; or acquired; the verb resembles Cain's name] a man. Abel took care of flocks, and Cain became a farmer [was a tiller/worker of the ground].

Genesis 4:1, 2b

Even after the disobedience of Adam and Eve, God didn't strip them of their procreative power. They *knew* each other and true to their nature, *made* a *living* being on the earth. They called him Cain. In Biblical times, naming a child was much like declaring a prophecy because the name reflected who the child would grow to become. Cain's name means "to produce" or "acquired." Like Adam, Cain was a husbandman by profession. *Produce* is defined as "gained by physical exertion" or "harvest." This could suggest that Cain was self-willed and relied upon his own strength to produce. Cain believed that he had the ability to yield a harvest at will. His rebellion is clear at harvest time when it was time to give God a sacrifice. God was not pleased with Cain. Genesis 4b-5a says:

> *And the Lord had respect (regard) for Abel and for his offering; but for Cain and his offering He had no respect.*

So why was Cain's offering considered evil and Abel's good (see 1 John 3:11-12)? Cain *was* called to produce fruit, so you'd think that God would've accepted his sacrifice. Delving deeper, there are several possible explanations why God despised his offering.

1. CAIN WAS LED BY HIS FLESH

*After that, Eve gave birth to Cain's brother
Abel [resembles the word for vapor or breath].*

Genesis 4:2a

Abel's name means "breath." When thinking of breath, *Ruach Ha'kodesh*, Holy Spirit, comes to mind. The Greek word for Spirit is *pneuma*, which means "to breathe," as when the breath of life came into Adam. Afterward, he became a living, breathing being. Without the Breath of Life, there is no existence. Because Abel's name means "breath," it is evident that he depended on the Spirit of God. From the word *pneuma* comes pneumonia. Pneumonia is a potentially deadly condition marked by an inability to breathe properly. It can be deduced that Cain had spiritual pneumonia. So God didn't accept Cain's offering because he had a chronic inability to be led by God's breath. Contrary to Cain, Abel didn't operate in self-will but in God's will. Abel didn't operate by the might of his arm or the power of his flesh, but by the Spirit of God (see Zechariah 4:6). While Cain produced from the fruit of his flesh, Abel functioned in the fruit of the Spirit.

2. CAIN GAVE GOD A CHEAP SACRIFICE

*Later [In due course; At the end of the days],
Cain brought some food [produce; fruit] from the
ground as a gift [tribute] to God. Abel brought
the best parts [fat portions;] from some of the
firstborn of his flock. The Lord accepted [looked
with favor on] Abel and his gift [tribute], but he
did not accept [look with favor on] Cain and his
gift [tribute].*

Genesis 4: 3-4, EXB

Scripture reveals that Cain gave God *some* "fruit of the soil" while Abel gave the *best of* "the firstborn of his flock." God's disapproval of Cain was also based upon the quality of the sacrifice. He made God an afterthought and in arrogance, gave a holy God mere leftovers. He put himself first, presenting a sacrifice that was second best.

3. CAIN DISOBEYED GOD'S INSTRUCTION

> *The Lord God made clothes from animal skins for the man [or Adam; 1:27] and his wife and dressed them.*

After Adam and Eve fell and were stripped from their coverings of glory, God covered them with animal skins. He established a precedent by killing an animal as a blood sacrifice for Cain's parents. Instead of adhering to this practice, Cain, embroiled in self-will, ill motives, and selfish ambition, gave God what he produced in disobedience. He didn't give God what was required of him.

Genesis 4:5b-7 continues:

> *So Cain became extremely angry (indignant), and he looked annoyed and hostile. And the Lord said to Cain, "Why are you so angry? And why do you look annoyed? If you do well [believing Me and doing what is acceptable and pleasing to Me], will you not be accepted? And if you do not do well [but ignore My instruction], sin crouches at your door; its desire is for you [to overpower you], but you must master it.*

Even after Cain gives a contemptible offering, God still speaks words of encouragement and warning to him. But instead of being repentant, Cain becomes indignant. He insulted God with his offering, but *he* had the audacity to become offended. And because of his attitude and clear objection to God's instruction, the sin introduced by his parents crouched at the door of his own heart. As an animal preparing to pounce on its prey, a sinful wicked plot jumped into the mind of Cain.

> *But people are [each person is] tempted when their own evil desire leads [lures; drags] them away and traps [entices; lures] them. This desire leads to sin [Then, after desire is conceived, it gives birth to sin], and then the sin grows [or becomes full-grown] and brings [gives birth to] death.*

> *James 1:14-15, EXB*

The envy and insolence of Cain accompanied by an evil, murderous desire gave birth to death and he killed his brother. But it doesn't end here. After Cain gave God a disgraceful sacrifice, after he ignored His instructions and even after he murdered Abel in cold blood, Cain persevered in his revolt.

> *The Lord said to Cain, "Where is Abel your brother?" And he [lied and] said, "I do not know. Am I my brother's keeper?*

> *Genesis 4:9*

Cain told an outright lie to the Creator of the Universe. He lied to the One who knew his heart and his motives yet loved him still. And he did so in the most reprehensible manner, by refusing to answer. However, even in death, Abel reverentially responded to the voice of his Creator. The voice of his blood cried out from the ground and reached the ears of God (see Genesis 4:10). The word "blood," as used in Genesis 4 refers to the seed Abel would never have the opportunity to sow in the earth; his posterity. In killing Abel, Cain killed Abel's descendants. As a result, read his fate in Genesis 4:11:

> *When you cultivate the ground, it shall no longer yield its strength [it will resist producing good crops] for you; you shall be a fugitive and a vagabond [roaming aimlessly] on the earth [in perpetual exile without a home, a degraded outcast].*

As with Adam, the very ground that Cain was called to cultivate, the very ground that once produced crops would resist him because of the blood of his brother spilled upon it. While his responsibility was to till the ground, it would require physical exertion because of his indiscretions.

GOD REQUIRES OUR BEST.

Sacrifice is not a word that we like because it's often associated with something we must give up. We love discussing "the anointing," "the glory" and "the blessings" but without the sacrifice it requires. We simply cannot offer God our inferior sacrifice. He requires and deserves our absolute best. Also, when God gives us clear instructions on how to harvest our land, our response must be immediate submission. We mustn't function in prideful self-will, determining in our own hearts what is sufficient for Him. We should operate in the fruit of the Spirit and not yield from the fruit of our flesh.

God knows us at our core. He knows our intentions. He knows our motives. If we allow wicked desires to penetrate our hearts, we will kill everything God has blessed us with. Blood will be required on our hands if we do not complete our assignments in the earth (see Ezekiel 3:18). Because in doing so, we not only kill our destiny, but we affect the destinies of those tied up in our harvest.

Matthew 21 tells the parable of Wicked Husbandmen. The owner planted a vineyard and allowed husbandmen to rent there as he traveled. At harvest time, on multiple occasions, the owner sent servants to collect his portion of the harvest as payment. However, the husbandmen killed each of them. Finally, the owner sent his son reasoning that they would surely not kill him. He was wrong. Showing no regard, they murdered him as easily and willingly as they did the others. Those wicked husbandmen were sentenced to death; their places in the garden were given to those who were honest and would give to the owner the harvest due to him.

God gave the best sacrifice when He offered up His only begotten Son for us. There never was nor never will be a greater Sacrifice than Him (see Hebrews 12:4). We have an obligation to Him.

> Therefore, I tell you that the kingdom of God will be taken away from you and given to a people who will produce its fruit.
>
> Matthew 21:43

God has entrusted us in His plan to reap a harvest for kingdom purposes. Therefore, when we receive that harvest, we have the obligation of giving it back to Him. We must give Him what's due to Him and prove ourselves as worthy husbandmen. If not, God can raise up vessels of honor who have no problem giving Him the best of themselves. We must continually cultivate the garden of our hearts, so it doesn't grow stony or full of weeds. Tell God yes for real, then be ready for the sacrifice that your "yes" requires. He will be with you along the way.

There is a beautiful promise penned in Amos that I'd like to leave with you. It reads:

> *I will bring my people Israel back from captivity [exile]; they will build the ruined cities again, and they will live in them. They will plant vineyards and drink the wine from them; they will plant gardens [or orchards] and eat their fruit. I will plant my people on their land, and they will not be pulled out again [uprooted] from the land which I have given them," says the Lord your God.*
>
> *Amos 9:14-15*

PART TWO

A TIME TO BUILD UP

8

VESSEL OF WEALTH

DESTINY IS NOT FOR the faint of heart. It involves a ferocious fight and you must be brave to walk in it. Expect a battle for your identity and your mind. The enemy knows that if he can get you to forfeit who you are in your mind, you'll never become who God says you are in the earth. On numerous occasions, the enemy has tried to use my circumstances to contradict who God said that I was. It was during these times of uncertainty that I literally waged war with the promises; with the very dreams I was given. While I was strong enough to fight the devils of distraction, it's sad to think of how many have been buried with purpose, dreams, and visions because the enemy bewitched them. You must know who you are and remember what God has said about you in the midst of it all.

In a dream, I laid upon a table in a storehouse. God lifted me toward the ceiling. I heard Him speak, "I Am preparing you to go to the nations. Remember what I said about you, and don't allow men to speak lies into your life…" At the time in 2010, I didn't understand what this meant. But as I experienced life and decided to pursue and become who God said I was, I met resistance. It came in the form of human beings influenced by demonic forces. God was telling me to remember what He said when times were hard. It's easy to forget when everyone and everything around you contradict His voice. I was to pay no attention to what they thought but focus on what He knew.

> *Before I formed you in the womb I knew you [and approved of you as My chosen instrument], and before you were born I consecrated you [to Myself as My own]; I have appointed you as a prophet to the nations.*
>
> *Jeremiah 1:5*

God tells Jeremiah, "I formed you, I knew you, I approved you, I chose you, I set you apart, and I appointed you." And even though Jeremiah gives a rebuttal, it didn't matter because God had already formed His vessel based upon His knowledge. And after Jeremiah explained to God why he felt he wasn't qualified, God corrects him and tells him that he will do exactly what he was formed, approved, chosen, set apart and appointed to do. God *knew* Jeremiah. The Hebrew word for "knew" as it's used in the text above is *yada*, which means "to ascertain by seeing, observation, and care."

Imagine God lovingly gazing at us carefully in our purest state. Imagine His thoughts toward us before being assigned to a womb and before entering the filthy condescending world. Imagine God speaking words of destiny to our very core. Envision Him declaring over us who we have the potential to become then shaping us according to His divine blueprint. He gives us our voices, our personalities… our quirks, all the things we sometimes dislike about ourselves. After filling our wombs with destiny, the Master Creator fills our mother's womb with us. We're pregnant with purpose at birth. Our mother gives birth to our physical bodies, so we can give birth to our spiritual assignments. Still, the earth's cynicism remains. We come through the birth canal into a limited world with words of grandeur spoken over us by our limitless God. We're born into sin and shaped by iniquity, but eternity remains in our hearts (see Psalm 51:5).

At one point, not many believed what God said about me. My environment made me feel like less than nothing. Nothing was working. My circumstances were dire. But then I remembered that it wasn't about me or my feelings. There was an eternal promise inside of me. The enemy was not only attempting to kill me, but he desires to destroy all the destinies of those attached to my harvest. Sometimes God allows us to experience lack and suffer drought, so others can be fed (see 1 Kings 17:2-16). And if I couldn't fight for myself, at least I could fight for you. I learned that it's okay for people not to believe in me. It's okay for human beings to doubt what *God* said about *me*. With Jesus and I on one side of a room, and every other person in the world on the other, I am still with the majority. I was still major in the midst of the minor opinions of men.

You too must get to the place where you understand that if no one in this world trusts the vision God gave, it's okay because they didn't give it, nor did they receive it. Other human beings don't have the responsibility of believing or comprehending what God told *you* to do. Stand with your dream and never back down. There is something greater at stake than your emotions. God will allow your feelings to be hurt because your assignment is too great for you to be led by them. It's not about you; it's about the reason you were birthed into the earth with a limitless word. Awaken to what God spoke to you before the foundations of the earth. What He gave you was given in eternity. So, while human beings may attempt to humiliate, belittle, and berate you, they don't have the power to strip your mantle because it's already been established in your core.

> *He has also planted eternity [a sense of divine purpose] in the human heart [a mysterious longing which nothing under the sun can satisfy, except God]—yet man cannot find out (comprehend, grasp) what God has done (His overall plan) from the beginning to the end.*

> *Ecclesiastes 3: 11b*

The fertile ground of your heart has been planted with good seed. This seed of eternity has the potential to bring forth fruit of greatness. Eternity is crying out of your heart to become. Refuse to get lost on a path of discovering who you are according to the thoughts of humans. All you have to do is uncover what He said about you before you breathed your first breath; before you lost your limitless word to a limited population of people.

Is eternity speaking and you silence it? Is your limitless word of creativity attempting to make a cameo in modern day society, but you suppress it? What has God spoken to you about completing? Do you feel it's too big to accomplish? If God told you to do it, it will be. If you could handle it, it would be *your* vision, mission, or dream. Your dream must be limitless in order for it to be God. If you can accomplish it in your own strength, you don't need God's.

In Judges 6 we read a story of a seemingly gutless man named Gideon. We can find Gideon hiding in a winepress from harvest thieves when an angel calls him a brave, mighty warrior. Human beings and his actions reduced him to a coward, but God saw Gideon's substance. He looked past the outward distraction of cowardice and looked into Gideon's vessel and called the warrior forth to defeat the enemy of his harvest. Gideon came to himself—his true self—and conquered the Midianites, taking their spoil. Afterward, Gideon requested a gold ring from every warrior in his camp as payment. Requesting the gold wasn't the issue; it was what he created with the wealth.

Judges 8:27 says:

> *Gideon made [all the golden earrings into] an ephod [a sacred, high priest's garment], and put it in his city of Ophrah, and all Israel worshiped it as an idol there, and it became a trap for Gideon and his household.*

Gideon grew up feeling as though he was less than everyone else in his father's house (see Judges 6:15). And though God increased him, he relapsed into his less than mentality, gathered wealth, and literally made an idol of it. His blessings entrapped him.

If you're called to wealth harvesting, you will bring forth great riches. But we were created to be vessels of wealth not create vessels of idolatry from wealth. Because money amplifies your character, it is vital that you understand who you are and who you are not before it arrives. Who you are with no money, no friends, and no support will be who you are with riches and influence, only intensified. Money magnifies what you are at your core. If you doubt God when you're penniless, you'll doubt Him when you're rich. The only danger in this is that when you're wealthy, you can afford shiny idols and unfulfilling placebos to try to satisfy a place that only God can.

Placebos come in all shapes, forms, and prices. They can range from a 200,000-dollar shopping spree to a pair of 2,000-dollar shoes to a bag of two-dollar chocolate almonds. After God stripped me to nothing, I could no longer afford to purchase expensive shoes to fill the void when I felt empty. However, unbeknownst to me, I'd found another placebo—chocolate almonds and energy drinks. The day I could no longer afford my placebo, I broke down. It literally broke my heart, but why? God led me to Isaiah 55:1-3a which says:

> *If you are thirsty, come here; come, there's water for all. Whoever is poor and penniless can still come and buy the food I sell. There's no cost—here, have some food, hearty and delicious, and beverages, pure and good. I don't understand why you spend your money for things that don't nourish or work so hard for what leaves you empty. Attend to Me and eat what is good; enjoy the richest, most delectable of things. Listen closely and come even closer. My words will give life.*

I was using the placebo to do what only He could, heal my heart, and feed my soul. I'd unknowingly allowed a two-dollar bag of chocolate almonds to take the place of God in my heart. Where are your idols? Where are your placebos? Where do you run when you're hurting? I encourage you to look deeply within and search them out because the vessel God created you to be is to be filled by Him, not with unfulfilling placebos.

You have this treasure from God, we are like clay jars that hold the treasure [in clay jars]. This shows that the great [extraordinary; transcendent] power is from God, not for us.

2 Corinthians 4:7

God created you to accomplish something specific that only you can and in a way that only you were shaped to handle. More specifically, the Creator used life to shape you into a vessel that can hold wealth. But more than that, He saw that you were a vessel that He could use to pour wealth through to others.

You are only human, and human beings have no right to question God [Who are you, a mere human being, to talk back to God?]. An object [or a thing molded] should not ask the person who made it [molder], "Why did you make me like this?]"

Romans 9:20 EXB

Those of us who are led by God realize that we have no choice in who He says we are. It is God who creates vessels. He designs them and fills them in the way that *He* chooses. He shapes and molds them according to His vision. This is no easy process to endure because the potter's wheel uncovers everything inside of you that's damning to who you are destined to become.

If you've ever seen a potter at work, you know that the clay in which he uses is an unimpressive, ordinary lump of nothing. Looking at it, it appears as though nothing great could ever be constructed from such a bland chunk of mud. However, the potter's wheel is designed to shape the unassuming clay into something spectacular. This is accomplished by a process known as [15]throwing. By throwing the clay, it's made even. It is forced to the center of the wheel by applying pressure with the hands. This shaping process is continued until the vessel is formed into the vision of the potter.

I've often felt as though God was throwing me around. And in between being thrown, I've felt an immense amount of pressure being applied to my life. I couldn't understand why God allowed it. But I soon realized that the enemy I was fighting was on the level of the platform He ordained for me to walk upon. In essence, the pressure was needed so I could handle my future and be centered in His will.

> *The potter can make anything he wants to make [Doesn't the potter have authority over the clay?]. He can use the same clay [lump] to make one thing [vessel; pot] for special [honorable] use and another thing for daily [common; dishonorable] use.*

> *Romans 9:21, EXB*

God's will is uncovered on His wheel. Don't rush the process. There is untapped wisdom and innovativeness inside of you that cannot be held and released if your vessel is not in proper form. It takes much longer to mold an elegant vase than it does an ordinary pot. It takes much more precision, cutting, and pressure. It's not because an average cup is less than an expensive vase. It's just that they each serve distinct purposes. It's not beneficial to drink water from a vase, nor is it functional to place flowers in an ordinary cup.

1 Corinthians 3:8-9, KJV says:

Now he that planteth and he that watereth are one: and every man shall receive his own reward according to his own labour. For we are labourers together with God: ye are God's husbandry, ye are God's building.

God molds and fills each vessel according to His omniscience. We are only responsible for carrying and fulfilling our own portion.

GOLDEN OIL

Again, I asked him, "What are these two olive branches beside the two gold pipes that pour out the golden oil? He said, "These are the two who stand beside the Master of the whole earth and supply golden lamp oil worldwide."

Zechariah 4:11-12

God gave Zerubbabel the great task of rebuilding the temple. As with all God-given assignments, he experienced resistance and he was discouraged in his building efforts. Faced with obstacles, he was tempted to give up. As a result, the Lord sent His angels to interpret visions from heaven to encourage him in his pursuit. The angel explained that the two who poured out golden oil worldwide represented Zerubbabel and Joshua. They stood as anointed leaders graced with golden oil needed to accomplish God's purpose in the earth.

Resistance will come, but there is a golden anointing produced in the lives of those called to wealth harvesting. It is an anointing with the grace to pour out blessings of the King worldwide. You will work hand-in-hand with the Master of the Universe so that His will, will be done on earth as it is in heaven. You are already equipped. Everything you've been through has strengthened you for your golden assignment. It has made you more resilient and tough. There comes a time when we must stop going back and forth with diaper demons (low-level fights and issues). See, the enemy sends them to distract us away from building. We see a prime example of this with Nehemiah. God called him to rebuild the walls of Jerusalem. Like clockwork, opposition in the form of human beings emerged.

> When Sanballat the Horonite, Tobiah the Ammonite officer, and Geshem the Arab heard about it, they made fun of us and laughed at us. When Sanballat heard that we were rebuilding the wall, he became angry and was greatly incensed. Can they bring the stones back to life from those heaps of rubble—burned as they are."
>
> Nehemiah 2:19a, 4:1,2b

There are at least three enemies every kingdom builder will encounter in their efforts, Sanballat, Tobiah, and Geshem. The name Sanballat means "enemy in secret." When you are called to accomplish something great, Sanballats will rise against you. Sanballats come in the form of people you've called friend and family your entire life. They've done a great job disguising themselves as a person who is for you, but the thought of your success is too much for them to handle. As a result, they will throw darts of manipulation to push you down from your stance of building. There will also be Tobiahs whose name means "the Lord is good." They disguise themselves as those who serve God. Tobiahs often come in the ruse of "helping" when their sole purpose is to ensure you're never elevated into a position above theirs. They are relentless enemies who attempt to sabotage your vision by any means necessary. The third enemy you will see will be the Geshems. Geshem means "rainstorm." A rainstorm involves a period of destructive, strong wind and heavy rain. Matthew 27 describes the stability of two different foundations during a rainstorm in verses 24-25. It says:

> So everyone who hears these words of Mine and acts on them, will be like a wise man [a far-sighted, practical, and sensible man] who built his house on the rock. And the rain fell, and the floods and torrents came, and the winds blew and slammed against that house; yet it did not fall, because it had been founded on the rock.

Geshem is an enemy that will come with foundational accusations against what you're building. They challenge your vision claiming it to be erroneous. However, because you are building upon a sure foundation, winds may blow, and rain may fall, but you will stand. Stay in your position and continue your assignment.

The other day I drove down a familiar road that's normally busy with cars in front of me and behind me. However, this time I was the only one in the lane at a red light. For a second, I felt self-conscience and wondered if I was in the correct lane because no one was ahead of me and no one was behind me. Needless to say, I was going the right way. What I learned from that situation is that it doesn't matter who's not backing you. It doesn't matter who hasn't traveled the path you're on before you. God specializes in new things; You are called to blaze trails. Stay in your lane and don't move. Obey what God tells you even if it appears strange to those around you.

> Those who were rebuilding the wall and those who carried burdens loaded themselves so that everyone worked with one hand and held a weapon with the other.
> Nehemiah 4:17

One day I bombarded heaven with prayers of great fervor and passion. Because I'd been in the midst of a launch of psychological warfare instigated by the enemy, I fought ferociously. But after I prayed the Lord told me that prayer is not all about shouting at the heavens; it's also about listening for strategy. He told me that the devil was in his place now it was time for me to stand in mine.

Nehemiah didn't use warfare as a crutch or an excuse to stop building. He continued to build amid threats, mockery, and opposition. In fact, He responded to the threats by saying, "I am doing a great work and cannot come down. Why should I leave to come down to your level" (see Nehemiah 6:3)? The higher you go, the fiercer the opposition but you are too far up to climb down and address bottom dwellers. Your vessel was shaped for this. You've been blazed by the fire, you've been submerged in the deep; you've been crucified. Dead men don't argue. Realize that some things are beneath you now. There are texts, emails, phone calls and words you've got to ignore. There are some things that are no longer your level, therefore not worthy of your time. High platforms require high character.

THAT DEVIL'S NOT ON YOUR LEVEL.

Stop using bottom level warfare as an excuse to cease building what God ordained for you to build. Build in the midst of warfare. Build in the midst of doubt. Build in the midst of mockery. Build in the midst of shame. Pick up the weapon of the word God gave you with one hand but build with the other. Believe in who God ordained for you to be. Believe in your assignment and stand in your place. It is time to enter the dimension of wealth God carved your vessel to handle.

9

***

YOUR WEALTHY PLACE

GOD NEVER INTENDS FOR us to take up residence in our land of ruins. Every seed… your dream or vision that has gone into the ground and died, only died with the purpose to grow in a greater measure (see John 12:24). Your tears watered that fallen seed to produce a harvest of a greater anointing, influence, and the greater version of you needed to serve the greater good in a larger sphere. Your hardships created the capacity inside needed to match the land of wealth God designed for you to inhabit. "The training of God is painful while we endure them, but they produce a transformation of character, bringing a harvest of righteousness" (Hebrews 12:11).

In a dream, I saw myself walking through a desert, then through a storm, followed by torrential rain. I noticed that at the end of the path was a rainbow and a pot of gold. However, when I arrived at that pot of gold, I experienced intense invisible warfare. After fighting hand and fist for a while, the hand of God finally lifted me up from the midst of the warfare and put me on the other side where there was fertile, well-watered land. The fight I endured was worth what was waiting for me on the other side.

> *For You, O God, have tested us; You have refined us as silver is refined. You brought us into the net; You laid affliction on our backs. You have caused men to ride over our heads; we went through the fire and through the water; But You brought us into our wealthy place.*

> *Psalm 66:10-12*

Before the Lord brought the children of Israel out of suffering, they were brought *through* some difficult places. *God* led them into a net, a place where they felt trapped and immobile. *God* laid affliction on their backs—they experienced times where the burdens were so heavy that they felt they couldn't go any further. *God* also allowed men to "ride over their heads" producing mental and physical oppression. *God* brought them through the fire and through the water and it was *God* who led them into their "wealthy place." One version says He brought them "into a land that is rich and abundant." Though they'd suffered in a wilderness place, a place of lack, and nothingness, God who allowed it. He used affliction to usher His children from a season of travail into a place of promise.

I will drive them out before you little by little,
until you have increased and are strong enough
to take possession of the land.

Exodus 23:30

Before God can move around us, He has to move in and through us. And once He has enlarged the territory of our heart, He can enlarge the territory in our midst. The weight of oppression, the fire, and the rain served the perfect purpose of strengthening your core. Because it is then that you'll be strong enough to possess. Once the tool of affliction has served its purpose, God lifts it and then He lifts us into our places of wealth. There is a land flowing with abundance designed for the grace on your life. It is the place where a need in the earth and the abundance of you collide. It is the place where you produce a harvest of solutions from the harvest of trials you've endured. It is a place specifically designed for your feet to tread upon. Psalm 18:33&36 says it this way:

> *He makes my feet like hinds' feet [able to stand*
> *firmly and tread safely on paths of testing and*
> *trouble]; He sets me [securely] upon my high*
> *places. You enlarge the path beneath*
> *me and make my steps secure, so that my feet will*
> *not slip.*

Just as there are tests that are unique to you, there is also a path leading to your wealthy place unique only to you. The pain you've experienced qualify the "enlarged" path beneath you. If those who have not been tried and proven, attempt to follow, the path beneath them becomes narrow and dangerous.

In a dream, I saw a woman walking with her bare feet on diamonds. In all actuality, the diamonds should've cut her feet. However, upon closer inspection, I saw that the soles of her feet were protected by a thick layer of gold. As she continued to walk effortlessly, people attempted to follow her path. However, their feet were cut because they did not have the golden soles needed to navigate it. Ecclesiastes 7:12-13 says:

> *For together wisdom and money are alike in this: both offer protection from life's misfortunes, But the real advantage of this knowledge is this: wisdom alone preserves the lives of those who have it. Think for a moment about the work of God. Can anyone make straight what God has made crooked.*

As discussed earlier, money is important, but wisdom is necessary to navigate God ordained paths. This wisdom only comes by the experience of ruination. And because you will operate at a capacity of excellence with ease, your path will entice many.

YOUR FIERY TRIAL BLAZED YOUR GOLDEN TRAIL.

Sadly, some will attempt to copy your assignment. However, they fail to realize that because you have walked through the blazing fire, God has equipped you with golden soles. With them, you blaze trails and navigate systems that many cannot.

GIANTS IN YOUR LAND

There were Nephilim (men of stature, notorious men) on earth in those days- and also afterward when the sons of God lived with the daughters of men, and they gave birth to their children. These

were the mighty men who were of old, men of
renown (great reputation, fame).

Genesis 6:4

Some believe that the "sons of God" mentioned above refer to the descendants of Seth. Others believe that fallen angels slept with "daughters of men" and produced "giants" or "men of renown" called Nephilim in the land (see Jude 1:6). Whatever the case, giants called Nephilim existed, and they sought to intimidate God's people. Famous for their enormous stature, Nephilim excelled in strength and wickedness. During this time evil was and an all-time high; God regretted creating man. Fed up with the degradation, He decided to destroy the entire earth. However, mercy was found in the midst of His wrath. He raised up Noah to be a standard of righteousness in the earth.

Isaiah 59:19 says, "When the enemy shall come in like a flood, the Spirit of the Lord shall lift up a standard against him." *Standard*, as used above is *noos* which comes from the primitive word *flit*. Flit means to "move swiftly" to "vanish away," or "to put to flight." There are giants in the land that God ordained for you to occupy. There are wicked men of stature, men of fame, and men of fortune sitting in the places where God desires for you to sit. However, God has graced you with the ability to put them to flight. God is raising you to be a standard in a place where standards have been abandoned. Just as God called Noah to build in times where wickedness covered the earth, He is releasing you to institute something new and unheard of in the earth. As you go forth, those giants in your way will move quickly and vanish before your very eyes. You must establish in your heart and believe what God is saying. If you cannot see yourself in your wealthy place, you can't access it. The spies in the book of Numbers prove this point.

> *But the men who had gone up with him said, "We are not able to go up against the people [of Cannan] for they are too strong for us." So, they gave the Israelites a bad report about the land which they had spied out, saying "The land through which we went, in spying out, is a land that devours its inhabitants. And all of the men are of great stature. There we saw Nephilim and we were like grasshoppers in our own sight, and so we were in their sight.*

> *Numbers 13:31-33*

In the Word of God, the number twelve represents establishing an infrastructure in the earth. It represents a governmental foundation. So, God had already established the foundation of the promised land for the Israelites. It was a done deal. Yet ten of the twelve spies still saw themselves as "grasshoppers." Notice that it was only after they saw themselves as grasshoppers that the Nephilim saw them as grasshoppers as well. A grasshopper is a word that is often used to describe a "novice, a person of inexperience," or "a person young in knowledge." God called them possessors, yet they felt like novices. They served the God of infinite knowledge, yet they couldn't see past their flaws.

I'm a first generational preacher. I had no prior knowledge of writing books, creating wealth, or teaching others to do the same. I had to learn that God isn't concerned about our human limitations. He doesn't focus on our race, creed, or nationality. He's not intimidated by our age and socioeconomic status. While God uses our background, He's not limited by it. When He looks at us He doesn't see us based upon what we perceive as barriers. He is the Creator of the Heavens and the earth. He supersedes time and breaks barriers. But the first barrier He will break is the barrier blocking our minds from our true self. Don't allow giants in the industry to discourage and cheat you out of your destiny. Luke 12:11-12 reads:

> *When they bring you before the synagogues and the magistrates and the authorities, do not be worried about how you are to defend yourselves or what you are to say; for the Holy Spirit will teach you in that very hour what you ought to say.*

The wisdom of God in your heart advances you far beyond those in your sphere. Realize that God has equipped you with the grace and anointing needed to navigate the paths that many people die on. Keep the promises of God in your heart as you encounter territorial giants. Though intimidating, you have the golden soles needed to walk unlikely paths. As you walk, you'll open your eyes to see that the only giant left is you. You are the mogul. You are the heavyweight anointed to go into uncharted places. God endowed you with the power to endure the weight of wealth. God is saying to you today what He said to Joshua:

> *I have given you every place on which the sole of your foot treads, just as I promised Moses. No man will [be able to] stand before you [to oppose you] as long as you live.*
>
> *Joshua 1:3*

When you are given the mandate to enter your land, it is important that you enter with the correct mindset. You enter the land knowing it is only by His Spirit—not by your might or power—that you will carry out great feats for His kingdom (see Zechariah 4:6). You must know that no matter where you go, He goes.

After the Philistines had captured the ark of God, they took it from Ebenezer to Ashdod. Then they carried the ark into Dagon's temple and set it beside Dagon. When the people of Ashdod rose early the next day, there was Dagon, fallen on his face on the ground before the ark of the Lord! They took Dagon and put him back in his place. But the following morning when they rose, there was Dagon, fallen on his face on the ground before the ark of the Lord! His head and hands had been broken off and were lying on the threshold; only his body remained.

1 Samuel 5:1-4

The Philistines laid hold of the ark of God and sat it in the temple next to a false god. Dagon, the principal deity of the Philistines, was considered the "god of fertility and crops." It's interesting that God knocked the head and the hands off Dagon. The hands represent productivity and the head represents wisdom and knowledge. Dagon was already in position but when the Presence of God entered the room, it had to surrender to the Highest Authority.

As a wealth harvester, the knowledge God imparts will always supersede that of the giants in your territory. The Presence of God in your life will cause the giants to break, bow, and submit to the authority given to you. God will break the productivity and the fruitfulness of every person trying to occupy your land. The level at which you will operate will baffle many because like David, you have a secret weapon.

A champion named Goliath, who was from Gath, came out of the Philistine camp. His height was six cubits and a span. David said to the Philistine, "You come against me with sword and spear and javelin, but I come against you in the name of the Lord Almighty, the God of the armies of

Israel, whom you have defied. Reaching into his bag and taking out a stone, he slung it and struck the Philistine on the forehead. The stone sank into his forehead, and he fell face down on the ground. David ran and stood over him. He took hold of the Philistine's sword and drew it from the sheath. After he killed him, he cut off his head with the sword.

1 Samuel 17: 4, 45, 49-51

Here, yet another enemy from the Philistine camp is attempting to defy the name of the Lord. And again, we see that God raised up a standard by the name of David, equipped with only a rock and a sling to take him out. Though his weaponry was mock-worthy, David knew exactly where his power and his strength came from. He understood that he wasn't fighting with mere carnal weapons, but he was fighting with the name of the Lord. David's seemingly insignificant stone navigated by the Spirit of God struck Goliath's forehead. Instantly he fell.

The giants in your land operate in mere humanistic logic and ideology. They scoff at the wisdom of God. But in this season, God will remove giants and vindicate His people. He will pull down moguls. He will destroy every legalistic and religious mindset to get His wealth harvesters into position.

I have seen another restless evil in this world, the kind of error that arises from those in power: fools and their folly are promoted to positions of authority, while the rich and talented are assigned menial tasks. I have seen slaves riding on horseback like royalty and princes walking on the ground like slaves.

Ecclesiastes 10:5-7, VOICE

Many with self-proclaimed elitism serve as gatekeepers to platforms of prominence. As a result, their "favorites" are often pushed into titles and positions above those who are truly deserving. While human beings have the tendency to promote whoever they consider worthy, God's positioning is unlike the positioning of people. Once He places you, He plants you in an unmovable place. God has prepared a group of harvesters—a royal priesthood who will no longer walk the earth as slaves of the system but will come to the forefront and reign in their wealthy places.

10

THE SHAKEDOWN

WITH ONLY A HUNDRED miles of coastline for the entire state of Georgia, a hurricane is a rare, isolated event. In fact, since 1851, only twenty hurricanes have made direct hits in the state. Aside from Georgia only having 100 miles of coastland, that coastland includes over 400,000 acres of saltwater marsh. The marsh islands along the coast are called "barrier islands" because they often block ocean waves and wind from hitting the mainland. Further, Georgia is shaped in such a way that it is hidden from hurricanes, leaving Florida and the Carolina's more vulnerable to attack. It would seem that the state of Georgia is all but impenetrable. However, though an uncommon event, Georgia recently experienced *Hurricane Michael.*

Hurricanes begin as harmless tropical storms. It is only when the tropical storm encounters favorable conditions such as warm air and warm ocean water that it develops into a hurricane. Still, even after development, most hurricanes remain undamaging until they move toward land producing wind up to 320 miles per hour. Once a hurricane reaches land, it produces a "storm surge" which causes high winds and drives the sea toward the shore. This causes water levels to rise, creating large crashing waves and leaving a path of destruction and ruin on the earth.

Days prior to Hurricane Michael, with warnings of a stage four hurricane buzzing, the entire city was in chaos. Streets were crowded, grocery stores were filled to the max; lines at the gas station were the longest I'd ever seen. Some breathed a sigh of relief when forecasters announced that the hurricane was reduced from a level four to a level one. However, because of inexperience and uncertainty, most still didn't know exactly what to expect, including me. Even though I'd heard of the ruin ravished upon coastal regions before, experience remains the best teacher. And a few nights later that experience I'd gain. Because even with all of its protective barriers, a storm still emerged in Georgia.

Kneeled down in a closet, the eerie sound of the howling wind plagued me. As the earth shook around me the constant thumps of flying elements pummeled against the roof. After hours of darkness and uncertainty, the blackness of the storm faded into the light of day. After the storm, there were no luxuries, air conditioning, phone services, or running water. Outside was equally catastrophic. The level of destruction and ruin was alarming to say the least. It amazed me how in just a few hours, 30-foot trees, structures, and buildings that had existed for years were completely uprooted. Streets, homes, businesses, and landmarks were unrecognizable. The entire city would remain without electricity for weeks to come.

While I don't believe that God directly forms hurricanes and natural disasters on the earth to destroy His people, He remains sovereign, so if they happen, He allows them to. Deuteronomy 29:19, AMPC says:

> *And lest, when he hears the words of this curse and oath, he flatters and congratulates himself in his [mind and] heart, saying, I shall have peace and safety, though I walk in the stubbornness of my [mind and] heart [bringing down a hurricane of destruction] and sweep away the watered land with the dry.*

Deuteronomy 29:19, AMPC

Here God warns His people. If they persisted in their disobedience, there would be consequences. If they continued to walk in the stubbornness of their own minds and hearts, "hurricanes of destruction" would wreak havoc in their lives. Likewise, hurricanes of destruction are moving upon the face of the earth as a result of the disobedience and injustices taking place upon it. Romans 8:22 confirms and says, "for we know that the whole creation has been moaning together as in the pains of childbirth until now." Our land needs healing, but that healing won't come without humility and obedience.

Cali called my mom the other day. "Bring the Holy Ghost back," she demanded. Upon further investigation, we learned that she'd seen something big and white that quickly disappeared. When it disappeared she assumed someone had stolen it. We determined that she must've seen an angel and confused it with Holy Spirit. Though slightly misguided, her zeal impressed me and what she said stuck with me. It's time to bring the Holy Ghost back in all that we do on the earth. It is time to lay aside our works and listen to His voice as never before. It's time to covet His Presence and operate in righteousness.

Amos 8:7b-8a (EXB) warns:

> *I will never forget everything that these people did. The whole land [or earth] will shake because of it, and everyone who lives in the land will cry for those who died [mourn].*

Just as Hurricane Michael infiltrated the "safe" boundaries of Georgia, so will the world spheres occupied by those who defy the name of God. Lukewarm-ness has provided the appropriate climate for surges of justice to hit land. As unlikely as it may seem, hurricanes of destruction are developing in highly "shielded" places of influence that have never been hit before. And while God isn't the cause of the shaking, He will use it to bring forth justice in the earth. The people of God are being ravished, and it's time for His magistrates to rise and take their places. It's time to hear the cries of His people and serve as instruments of justice.

> *Now there was a great outcry of the [poorer] people and their wives against their Jewish brothers [to whom they were deeply in debt]. For there were some who were saying, "We, along with our sons and our daughters, are many; therefore allow us to get grain, so that we may eat and survive."*
>
> *Nehemiah 5:1-2*

Here we witness the all too familiar pattern of greed causing division between those calling themselves brother and sister. The nobles of the land were guilty of starving their own people for their own selfish gain. They were literally taking advantage of and stealing from those God commanded them to bless.

Nehemiah 5: 6,11,13 continues:

> *Then I was very angry when I heard their outcry and these words [of accusation]. Please, give back to them this very day their fields, their vineyards, their olive groves, and their houses, and also a hundredth part of the money, the grain, the new wine, and the oil that you are lending them. I also shook out the front of my garment and said, "So may God shake out every man from his house and from his possessions who does not keep this promise; like this may he be shaken out and emptied.*

Nehemiah, enraged by their insatiableness, charged them to turn from their ways. He further told them to restore the gardens, vineyards and olive trees that were taken from their own people. And if they did not comply, they would come face to face with a financial curse; God would "shake their pockets empty." Proverbs 21:15 says, "When justice is done, good [righteous] people are happy, but evil people are ruined."

James 5:2 says:

> *Your wealth has rotted and is ruined and your [fine] clothes have become moth-eaten.*

It's one thing to be divinely ruined by the Lord; It's entirely different to be ruined by your own schemes.

After Hurricane Michael, the city began its stages of rebuilding. However, efforts would be frustrated as approximately one month after Hurricane Michael, a tornado tore through the city. Initially, the forecast revealed that the tornado would happen during the day. Many were relieved when it appeared to have dissipated, or so we thought. At approximately three in the morning, I was told to take cover. A tornado was on the land.

> When it is evening, you say, 'It will be fair weather, for the sky is red.' And in the morning, 'It will be stormy today, for the sky is red and has a threatening look.' You know how to interpret the appearance of the sky, but cannot interpret the signs of the times?
>
> Matthew 16:3

I'd awakened throughout the night by the sound of violent wind and lightning but thought nothing of it. I neglected the signs of an impending tornado because I was told by forecasters the storm wasn't coming. We, as the people of God, have the obligation to discern the times that we are in. We can no longer afford to sit idly as the world starves to death. We must open our eyes the poverty and stop shying away from the lack. Justice must be executed, and it will come through your hands and feet on the earth. We must work according to His plan while it is day because when night comes no man can work (see John 9:4).

> Israel's foolish plans are like planting the wind [They sow the wind], but they will harvest a storm [and reap the whirlwind]. Like a stalk with no head of grain, it produces nothing [no flour]. Even if it produced something, other nations [foreigners] would eat [devour] it.
>
> Hosea 8:7, EXB

Even now, many are guilty of breaking covenant with God and chasing after the desires of their own hearts. Forsaking Him, they prided themselves in their ability to build and grow. Like Cain, they use the strength of their own flesh and are guilty of constructing according to their own blueprints. At will, their flesh produces a manmade harvest. However, much like Israel sowed the wind and reaped a tornado, God is sending whirlwinds to uproot every structure that He didn't endorse. All efforts facilitated without Him will end in ruin and a spoiled harvest. God is shaking down everything that started and ended in the flesh.

> *In a short time, I will once again shake the heavens and the earth, the sea, and the dry land. I will shake all the nations, and they will bring their wealth the treasures of the nations shall come].*

> *Haggai 2:6, EXB*

Though the earth has quaked and shook as a result of sin and injustice, a heavenly shakedown is about to take place. God is shaking the pockets of the wicked managers of the earth; those in key positions who refuse His voice. He is shaking every sphere of this world for His glory. Hurricanes of Justice are being released upon every infrastructure and every foundation that's not founded upon the sure foundation of Jesus Christ. Those who have been guilty of raping people for money will be shaken out of place to make room for those who God is calling forth.

A shakedown is defined as "a radical change or restructuring in a hierarchal organization or group." As God shakes the earth—the spheres of this world— He will remove those out of position and shake the heavens to release resources that belongs to His harvesters. Haggai 2:21 (Message) says it best below:

I am about to shake up everything, to turn everything upside down and start over from top to bottom—overthrow governments, destroy foreign powers, dismantle the world of weapons and armaments, throw armies into confusion, so that they end up killing one another.

We are entering a season of the divine exchange where the wealth of the wicked will begin to pour into the kingdom as never before. Those operating in a golden anointing will be seated in their high places. They will shatter barriers, break through glass ceilings, and take over earthly spheres for the glory of God. Those who have their eyes set on a vision, with an unshakable foundation given by the Divine Architect and Builder will come forth and shake things up in the world (see Hebrews 11:10).

A DIVINE SHAKEDOWN IS TAKING PLACE.

Many months after the hurricane and the tornado ravished Georgia, I saw a *Disaster Relief* truck cleaning up leftover debris from the storms. It amazed me that after so long, residual effects remained, and clean-up efforts were still necessary. Disaster relief is defined as "responding to catastrophic ruin, providing aid and support for rebuilding efforts." It involves immediate intervention for the restoration of infrastructures.

They shall build up the ancient ruins; they shall raise up the former devastations; they shall repair the ruined cities, the devastations of many generations.

Isaiah 61:4

Divine disaster relief is on the way. Though it appears as though your life has been in ruins for far too long and it feels like you've been in this process forever, the cleanup was necessary. The Husbandman has torn you down and raised you up for such a time as this. And now that He has cleaned you up and molded you into an honorable vessel, it's time for restoration. It's time to rebuild organizations of wealth. Divine strategies are being released from heaven because you have been given the mandate to build. The Lord of the Harvest is calling you to arise and infiltrate.

11

DIVINE INFILTRATION

THE BATTLE WE ARE fighting is one in the heavens. It is a war of good versus evil, heaven versus hell, and its bounty is a wealth of souls. Using the spheres of this world, the enemy plants seeds of corruption. He taints minds and blinds eyes away from the Truth. In many instances, depravity and lewdness have become commonplace; truth and holiness is disdained and viewed as antiquated. The enemy would like for us to believe that he is winning. However, we know that Jesus has already won. Because He won, we win. So while it is the nature of the enemy to kill, steal, and destroy, it is our nature as believers to decree, trample, and overcome (see

John 10:10; Luke 10:19). Jesus has already overcome the world, and we are called to serve as light, bringing others into the knowledge of Him. Thus, we engage, and we fight for Truth because whether or not we acknowledge it, we are either dominating or being dominated by the world spheres around us.

The word *sphere* comes from the Greek word *metron* which means a "determined extent," or a "portion measured off." God in His wisdom appropriates a portion or sphere for each of His servants to dominate (see 2 Corinthians 10:13). It is within these spheres where a fierce battle ensues.

> *We know that we belong to God [or are children of God; are of God], but the Evil One controls the whole world.*
>
> *1 John 5:19, EXB*

Ephesians 2:2 describes Satan as the "prince of the power of the air" because he heavily influences the seven spheres (also called mountains or systems) of society. World spheres include religion, family, education, government, media, arts &entertainment, and business. The enemy positions his children in spheres to bring forth disgrace and "fight against the purposes of God" (see Ephesians 2:2). God positions His children to show forth His grace and fight against darkness. And though these spheres appear to be controlled by worldly influence, this does not override the "go ye" mandate given to us by Jesus. The prince of this world is after souls; so are we. We are after souls for the kingdom of God. Second Corinthians 10:4-5 reminds us that:

> *The weapons of our warfare are not physical [weapons of flesh and blood]. Our weapons are*

divinely powerful for the destruction of fortresses. We are destroying sophisticated arguments and every exalted and proud thing that sets itself up against the [true] knowledge of God, and we are taking every thought and purpose captive to the obedience of Christ.

We are called to destroy "sophisticated arguments," which means those operating in world spheres are by no means unintelligent. You'll find spheres occupied by intellectuals who operate at elevated levels, high IQ's, and capacities with a strong work ethic. However, no matter how sophisticated an individual is—without God—that person remains at a terrible disadvantage. Even when the world operates at its highest level of wisdom, it's still stupidity to God (see 1 Corinthians 3:19). The foolishness of God is wiser than man's wisdom (1 Corinthians 1:25). His thoughts and ways are infinitely greater, wider, and superior to that of His creation (see Isaiah 55:8-9).

In a dream, I saw a Christian mogul racing side by side with a worldly mogul to take her place. This dream showed me that there's a changing of the guards taking place. In response to Solomon's disobedience, God raised up Jeroboam in his stead. Jeroboam means "an oversized wine bottle with a capacity to hold four times more than an ordinary bottle." God is raising up anointed moguls on the earth with influence greater than those who allow their flesh to guide them. Because they have been with God, they have increased capacity and can hold and pour forth His wisdom in this earth. They understand spiritual matters and house an arsenal of spiritual wealth needed for the fight.

For our struggle is not against flesh and blood [contending only with physical opponents], but against the despotisms, against the powers, against [the master spirits who are] the world rulers of this present darkness, against the spiritual forces of wickedness in the heavenly (supernatural) sphere.

Ephesians 6:12

To be clear, our underlying issue is not the president of the United States. Our underlying issue is not racism. Our underlying issue cannot be traced back to mere human hands. Those are merely physical symptoms of the spiritual disease launched in the earth by the evil one. The evil we will face as we infiltrate isn't flesh and blood; they are powers, principalities, and rulers of spiritual wickedness that rule over the spheres of society. We cannot fight spiritual battles with physical weapons. Our weapons are spiritual. Our weapons are powerful. Our weapons are mighty.

THE WEAPON INSIDE SILENCES THE CHAOS
OUTSIDE.

The weapons of our warfare are divinely powerful and destroy "fortresses." A fortress is another word for "stronghold." Spiritually, strongholds are often ideas, thought patterns, traditions, or lies that hold an individual's mind captive and thus inhibit his walk. While the enemy rules in world systems, the earth and the fullness thereof still belong to God (see Psalm 24:1). And as believers, we have the authority to make spiritual transactions in the heavenly realm to manifest earthly changes. Our powerful weapons give us the ability to destroy exalted, high things that sets itself up against the knowledge of Christ. This means that structures that have been in place for years must go. Some who have been in positions for eons will be removed. Those who have been on the top of the mountains of society will crumble. The weapon of power in our hands will break through tradition with secret things breathed to us by God's Spirit. As we advance, we will take captive strongholds that have had eyes blinded for years. As we enter spheres, we snatch back those who belong to God from the gates of hell and from the clutches of the wicked one.

> *There was a man there named Zacchaeus. He was the chief tax collector in the region, and he had become very rich. When Jesus came by, he looked up at Zacchaeus and called him by name. "Zacchaeus!" he said. "Quick, come down! I must be a guest in your home today. Zacchaeus quickly climbed down and took Jesus to his house in great excitement and joy. But the people were displeased. "He has gone to be the guest of a notorious sinner," they grumbled. Meanwhile, Zacchaeus stood before the Lord and said, "I will give half my wealth to the poor, Lord, and if I have cheated people on their taxes, I will give them back four times as much!"*
>
> *Luke 1,5-8*

Religious busybodies watched as Jesus sat with tax collectors and prostitutes and accused Him of compromising. They didn't understand that He came for the sick, not the presumably whole (see uke 5:31). Jesus operated in a dimension of kingdom expansion, not in a spirit of elitism. Zacchaeus was hated by many, especially the Pharisees. However, Jesus looked into his core; He knew his nature. Zacchaeus means "clean and pure." So while religious hypocrites saw a filthy tax collector, Jesus saw a pure kingdom philanthropist willing to give back half of his wealth and four times what he stole. One meeting with a "notorious sinner," produced a kingdom wealth harvester. God is not calling us to compromise, but He is requiring us to "go ye" into the world and minister to the spiritually impoverished. For some, this will require sitting in places other than prayer brunches, church pews, and Christian conferences. The wealth of the *wicked* is laid up for the just (Proverbs 13:22). We quote that Scripture, but do we really comprehend it? If so, we know that God has laid aside wealth for His kingdom, but He didn't say He laid it in the church. It belongs to the kingdom, but it's being used by the world to promote evil agendas. In the words of Caleb in Numbers 13:30, "let us go up at once and take possession of it; for we will certainly conquer it."

As I thought about what to name this chapter, the word "infiltration" immediately came to mind. *Infiltration* is a military term which means "to pass through weak places in the enemy lines, gradually, to seize control from within." One of my favorite synonyms for infiltration is "permeate."

Matthew 13:33 (NLT) says:

> *The Kingdom of Heaven is like the yeast a woman used in making bread. Even though she put only a little yeast in three measures of flour, it permeated every part of the dough.*

Elsewhere in the Word of God, leaven or yeast denotes evil influence or false doctrine. However, in this Scripture, the leaven represents a small beginning or a small entrance of the Word of God. When the leaven enters through the small entrance, it permeates the entire loaf. In warfare, infiltration involves small independent light infantry forces advancing into enemy rear and bypassing the enemy frontline strongpoints. To infiltrate is also "to gradually gain access to an organization or place specifically to take over to influence the way it behaves."

One morning, I noticed a tiny green sprout growing between concrete in the driveway. I wondered how that minuscule, insignificant plant could grow in a place that seemed unlikely. How was it able to push through concrete? It was simple. It couldn't.

> *The whole earth sprouts newness and life in the springtime, and green shoots break through the well-seeded garden soil. That's what it is like with the Eternal's victory— the Lord will cause justice and praise to sprout up before all the nations, for all peoples to see.*
>
> *Isaiah 61:11*

The sprout didn't break through the concrete. There were roots that already existed in the ground beneath it. When it rained, the sprout was watered, and it infiltrated the cracks.

How does this apply to us? There are cracks in the spheres of this world; God will cause His wealth harvesters to sprout up and arise in territories that seem improbable. All it takes is one small issue in the world and one solution from God to infiltrate otherwise impenetrable domains. The world is feeble without God. No matter how strong an organization is, no matter how great a movie is, no matter how good a business is—without God—there are weak points. Those weak points are where we infiltrate with the manifold wisdom of God. We enter with creative power unseen and unheard of. God is releasing a small hidden remnant with deep roots to infiltrate world systems and permeate them with His Presence, thus changing the way the system behaves. Get ready to permeate rooms that aren't attached to a church. Get ready to permeate tables that aren't located in the fellowship hall. God is calling us to intrude and subdue. Now is not the time to sit around, hold hands, and sing "kum ba ya" because the violent take it by force (see Matthew 11:12).

Luke 19:12-13 (KJV) says:

> ...*A certain nobleman went into a far country to receive for himself a kingdom, and to return. And he called his ten servants, and delivered them ten pounds, and said unto them, Occupy till I come.*

A familiar parable, we know that the nobleman asks each one he'd invested in about their return. One servant produced ten bags of gold from the ten he was given, another produced five and one other faithful servant produced two bags of gold. Finally, there was one servant who was given one bag of gold. This servant failed miserably and was dealt with harshly. His fate is similar to the servant's fate in Matthew 25. It reads:

> *I was afraid and went and hid your money [talent] in the ground. [See] Here is your bag of gold [what is yours]. [But] The master answered, 'You are a wicked and lazy servant! You say you knew that I harvest things [reap where] I did not plant [sow] and that I gather crops where I did not sow any seed. So you should have put my gold [money]in the bank. Then, when I came home, I would have received my gold [what was mine] back with interest.*
>
> *Matthew 25:24-25*

To *occupy* is "to take possession and control a place by infiltration." The servant was harshly scolded because of his fear and lack of initiative to enter in a sphere where he was given access. He had the seed of wealth in his hands needed to infiltrate and produce a harvest but allowed fear to immobilize him. There is a difference between hiding a seed superficially in the ground and planting one. Planting produces a harvest;

hiding yields judgment. Fear is not an option when building; we operate in faith because we depend on God for the design.

> *It is He (God) who reveals the profound and hidden things; He knows what is in the darkness, And the light dwells with Him.*

> *Daniel 2:22*

King Nebuchadnezzar had a dream that only Daniel could repeat and interpret. The light of God illuminated the answer at the exact time that he needed it. He had the ability to uncover Nebuchadnezzar's secret.

> *The king answered Daniel and said, "Most certainly your God is the God of gods and the Lord of kings and a revealer of mysteries, since you have been able to reveal this mystery! Then the king promoted Daniel [to an exalted position] and gave him many great gifts, and he made him ruler over the entire province of Babylon and chief governor over all the wise men of Babylon.*

> *Daniel 2:47-48*

Because of the revealed mysteries of God, Daniel was exalted to a favored position within a sphere governed by a wicked ruler. He infiltrated and influenced an otherwise impermeable sphere with the secrets of God. His light so permeated the sphere that even Nebuchadnezzar—lover of Baal—could see that God is the God of all gods. He had to admit that inside of Him lies mysteries that *He* only reveals to *His* children.

As His child, there are secret things that only belong to you (see Deuteronomy 29:29). There are ideas that God has kept for thousands of years only for you. At the perfect moment, God will unveil solutions in every sphere of society where He plants

His children. Kingdom administrators are arising with an answer. No longer will you be in the background; the secret is getting ready to be revealed. Wealth harvesters equipped with wisdom, bruises from the battle and the Word of God will infiltrate in power and in might. They will be seen in high places of influence seated beside government officials, politicians, celebrities, and musicians.

In a dream I had many years ago, I saw a celebrity in a beautiful garden at a wedding. She turned at the altar and said, "It's a beautiful time to build." I agree. It's a beautiful time to build upon the kingdom. It's a beautiful time to fulfill your destiny. It's a beautiful time to arise and expand to the left and the right. Even as I type this, I'm hearing "it's a beautiful time to be in the kingdom."

In another dream, I watched a pastor as he stood with about ten church members. He decided that it was time to build a new church because the one they were in wasn't up to par. As the pastor held a blueprint of the new church design, they were suddenly standing in front of the new building. The members couldn't see the new building that was right before them. They were too focused on limitations. They were concerned that there weren't enough of them to build but the pastor was unmoved by their doubt. Overnight, the building was up and full.

> *Those who wait for perfect weather [watch the wind] will never plant seeds [sow]; those who look at every cloud will never harvest crops.*
>
> *Ecclesiastes 11:4*

It won't always look like the right time to build. Look beyond the rain and the clouds. Look beyond the confusion and the doubt. You mustn't be afraid to step out and build when God gives you the clearance to build. Trust the blueprint He has placed in your hands. You can't look at your lack. You must look at His fullness and move in His divine timing or else you will never see your harvest. We will be held accountable for the wealth and territory God has laid in our care, yet we relinquished in fear.

I will offer one warning. As divine elevation takes place in your life, you must realize your worth in Him.

> *And He raised us up together with Him [when we believed], and seated us with Him in the heavenly places, [because we are] in Christ Jesus, [and He did this] so that in the ages to come He might [clearly] show the immeasurable and unsurpassed riches of His grace in [His] kindness toward us in Christ Jesus [by providing for our redemption].*
>
> *Ephesians 2:6-7*

Remember that your seat in the high place in your sphere reflects your seat in the high place with the Lord. Before you were ever seated in high places of wealth, God seated you in high places of immeasurable riches in Jesus. The riches of His grace keeps you. Remember the God who blessed you. Daniel was wise enough to remember. Joseph was wise enough to remember. Solomon in all his wisdom was not. The higher you go, the more difficult the issues. The higher you go, the costlier your mistakes. The higher you go, the further back down you have to fall.

As we infiltrate, success is certain. What's also certain is that the enemy will form devices to attempt to draw you away from God. Matthew 4 describes when Jesus was led into the wilderness. Satan came to tempt Him. Initially, he aimed to force Jesus to prove Who He Was (see Matthew 4:3). Jesus fought him with the Word. When the enemy couldn't force Jesus to prove His identity, he tried to make Him commit suicide (see Matthew 4:6). Again Jesus fought him with the Word. Then the devil took Jesus to a very high mountain/sphere (see Matthew 4:8). Satan attempted to get Jesus to bow down to him for position. Jesus, already seated at the highest position, once more, fought him with the Word.

> *So stand firm and hold your ground, having tightened the wide band of truth (personal integrity, moral courage) around your waist and having put on the breastplate of righteousness (an upright heart), and having strapped on your feet the gospel of peace in preparation [to face the enemy with firm-footed stability and the readiness produced by the good news]. Above all, lift up the [protective] shield of faith with which you can extinguish all the flaming arrows of the evil one. And take the helmet of salvation, and the sword of the Spirit, which is the Word of God.*

The enemy of your soul will come to tempt and test you. When he can't manipulate your assignment, he will try to kill you. If he can't kill you, he will attempt to enlist you. But like Jesus, we must fight. Our spiritual arsenal includes fighting from a stance of salvation in integrity, uprightness, stability, and faith. But the Word of God is our sword that takes the enemy out (see Hebrew 4:12). It must be planted in our hearts! It is our number one weapon. It speaks when we can't. It imparts wisdom. It reveals secrets and hidden mysteries needed to combat wickedness.

This world with all its shiny toys and bright lights are alluring, and its strategies are strong. So, we mustn't be ignorant of them (see 2 Corinthians 2:11). Your charge is to permeate kingdoms of darkness with light. You mustn't allow darkness to permeate your heart. I devoted the next section to two devices the enemy uses against those ordained to wealth.

1. THE SPIRIT OF MAMMON

Money has the potential to be worshiped; Therefore, it also has the potential to become an idol inside the heart. The children of Israel were all too familiar with this. They looked enviously at the wealth of neighboring pagan countries. As if the blessings of God were not enough, they lusted after theirs. In their disillusioned minds, idolatry reaped far greater benefits. The wealth of the world must never be regarded as greater than God. All material possessions gained outside of His will leads to death. Our confidence should be placed in God and in Him alone. He is our Source, not our "things."

> *No one can serve two masters; for either he will hate the one and love the other, or he will be devoted to the one and despise the other. You cannot serve God and mammon [money, possessions, fame, status, or whatever is valued more than the Lord].*

> *Matthew 6:24*

The word *mammon* is translated as "confidence, wealth, personified, and avarice." Avarice is defined as "reprehensible acquisitiveness, the insatiable desire for wealth." Avarice is impossible to satisfy. Mammon is a spirit with the insatiable desire to continuously obtain more. It is the driving force behind greed and lust. Mammon causes notable business associates to fight and outstanding members of society to go to prison for embezzlement. It is the devil behind wars, the instigator of divorce, and even murder. There is always a driving desire to get more, and the end is destruction.

> *You prostituted yourself with the Assyrians because you were not satisfied; you prostituted yourself with them and still were not satisfied. Men give gifts to all prostitutes, but you give your gifts to all your lovers, bribing the pagan nations to come to you [as allies] from every direction for your obscene immoralities.*

Ezekiel 16:28, 33

Israel was never satisfied. They had become so corrupt that they no longer took material possessions from their neighboring countries. Instead, they were so influenced by immorality that they paid neighboring countries to become their allies. Still, the desire for material wealth is a diversion from the underlying evil agenda of the spirit of mammon.

Mammon is said to be the Syrian "god of riches" and originated from Babylon. Another word used to define mammon is "deified," which means "to make a god of." The spirit of mammon along with pride is what influenced Nimrod to spearhead the construction of the Tower of Babel. The motivation behind building was to ascend into a position high enough to replace God. Nimrod's tower was not built to obtain material wealth; money is the distraction from the greater evil. It was built so that they could "make names for themselves" in the heavens. Babylon is the center of false doctrine and mammon plays an integral part in its construction. Because Babylon constructed the false belief system, those used by the spirit of mammon can excel in what they consider "spiritual wealth" and lead the multitudes astray. The spirit of mammon has persuaded many to take on the mentality of Nimrod, which says, "Let us build so that we can have great names."

While the wealth of the world is temporal, there is a greater wealth we as the people of God should seek after. We must not become so enamored by temporal pleasures that we forsake the eternal things of God. True wealth is and always will be found in God. No matter what sphere we infiltrate, our aim should never be to make names for ourselves. God will make your name great only so those you're to influence will glorify His. When it becomes more about us and less about Him, we've commenced building upon an already lucrative yet impoverished Babylonian world system.

2. THE SPIRIT OF POVERTY

We serve a God of opulence. He Is a God of immeasurable wealth. In Him is everything, there are no voids, no emptiness. In Him is the fullness and complete measure of existence. He is the King of kings and the Lord of lords. His kingdom and rule has no end (see Luke 1:33, Isaiah 9:7). He is the First and the Last, the Beginning and the End. He is the Alpha and the Omega and everything that is holy and pure and lovely originates in Him. He "owns cattle on a thousand hills" (see Psalm 50:10). He makes walls of jasper, cities of gold then decorate them with every precious stone to be imagined. He throws sapphires, diamonds, onyx, topaz, and pearls around like confetti. He paves streets with gold and panels floors with crystal. From Genesis to Revelation, the splendor of His glory is on full display, not hidden or disdained. Everything of beauty began with Him. So, how could a God capable of creating great opulence, splendor, and wealth have a kingdom of poverty and lack? It's simple, He cannot.

While the Bible speaks explicitly about God's devotions and love of the economically poor, poverty is never to be equated with holiness. In fact, it is often considered a curse to be broken. So, while God doesn't want us to fall victim to mammon, He doesn't want us to wallow in poverty either. Resolve in your mind that as a wealth harvester, God needs you wealthy. It is in your mind where God needs you to be wealthy first. Poverty begins in the mind; impoverished mindsets are damning.

> *The Midianites were so cruel that the Israelites made hiding spaces for themselves in the mountains, caves, and strongholds. Whenever the Israelites planted their crops, marauders from Midian, Amalek, and the people of the east would attack Israel camping in the land and destroying crops as far away as Gaza. And they stayed there until the land was stripped bare.*

> *Judges 6:2-3, 5b, NLT*

Israel was reduced to starvation and poverty because they were not equipped to stand against the enemy of their harvest. In fear of the Midianites—whose name means strife and warfare—the Israelites hid in caves of depression. A stronghold of poverty gripped their minds. The enemy comes to kill seed. He will send a spirit of death to steal and destroy the harvest. He will attempt to kill every bit of purpose that God has prepared for us if we are not prepared in our minds. If your mindset is not renewed, you will always be spiritually famished.

Luke 18 tells of a young wealthy ruler. He prided himself in keeping the law; he followed all the rules. He was successful and powerful. He was exuberantly wealthy in materialistic possessions. He had it all. Or at least he thought he did. Have you ever met the rich person who collects toys and trinkets, cars, and candy and once he has it "all" he's on a voyage for a new, temporary high? It is my belief that the ruler had no sincere desire to follow Jesus. He only wanted to add Him to his collection. However, you can't place an eternal God inside of a temporal toy box. You cannot confine the Savior of the universe to a gift box to pull and enjoy at leisure.

> *When Jesus heard this, He said to him, "You still lack one thing; sell everything that you have and distribute the money to the poor, and you will have[abundant] treasure in heaven; and come, follow Me [becoming My disciple, believing and trusting in Me and walking the same path of life that I walk]."*

> *Luke 18:22*

Jesus corrected the young ruler. Jesus saw past the wealth and past the superficial obedience and hit the young ruler at the heart of his issue, which happened to be in his pockets. The fact is that he was excessively rich and excessively poor at the same time. He had possessions but lived in a spirit of poverty. How do I know? Read below how he responded.

> *When he heard these things, he became very sad, for he was extremely rich. Jesus looked at him and said, "How difficult it is for those who are wealthy to enter the kingdom of God! For it is easier for a camel to go through the eye of a needle than for a rich man [who places his faith in wealth or status] to enter the kingdom of God."*

> *Luke 18:23-25*

This verse leads some to believe that Jesus looked down on the rich. No, He didn't pity those who had wealth; He pitied those who wealth had. There is a vast difference between the mindsets of the individual who uses wealth and the one that wealth uses. One is a harvester; the other is a slave. Because the young ruler put his faith in his status and money, there wasn't enough room in his heart for Jesus. Where your faith lies, your heart follows.

> *So then, none of you can be My disciple who does not [carefully consider the cost and then for My sake] give up all his own possessions.*
>
> *Luke 14:33*

Following Jesus will cost you everything. That was a price the ruler found too high to pay. He'd been given a strategy to break the spirit of poverty from his life but refused. He'd be required to give away all of his trinkets. Even with billions in hand, if what you own causes you to lose your soul and deny Jesus, you're broke. "Life is not measured by how much one owns" (Luke 12:15). If only the young ruler had known that whatever he lost for the sake of Jesus would be multiplied in his life.

> *Peter said, "Look, we have left all [things— homes, families, businesses] and followed You." And He said to them, "I assure you and most solemnly say to you, there is no one who has left house or wife or brothers or parents or children for the sake of the kingdom of God, who will not receive many times as much in this present age and in the age to come, eternal life."*
>
> *Luke 18:28-30*

Peter becomes concerned and reminds Jesus of his sacrifice. Jesus, in turn, reminds Peter that no one who sacrifices for His sake would lack in heaven or on earth. It's impossible to sacrifice for the sake of the kingdom and remain in a deficit.

> *... So that we do not offend them, go to the sea, and throw in a hook, and take the first fish that comes up; and when you open its mouth, you will find a shekel. Take it and give it to them [to pay the temple tax] for you and Me."*
>
> *Matthew 17:27*

Jesus didn't spiritualize Peter's physical needs. He pulled answers from the Spirit and manifested them in the natural. He produced the money at will and in the most unorthodox way— from the very mouth of a fish. Although Jesus came to earth with no material possessions and even though He had nowhere to lay His head, He never lacked anything. Everything He needed He created because He is the Word of God.

Physical money must be transacted in the physical world. So how do we manifest the wealth in our earthen vessels into the earth? By giving Jesus your "everything." By surrendering and allowing Him to break the spirit of poverty off. Allow Him to heal you so the enemy will find no poor place in you.

The spirit of poverty comes to reduce who you are. It comes to break and destroy legacies. It comes to cut off posterity and ruin destinies, but Jesus has come that we have life more abundantly (see John 10:10). But in order to have an abundant life, you must have a mind of abundance. Who you are on the inside will eventually manifest on the outside. Meaning that if you have an impoverished soul, your life will soon follow. On the contrary, if your mind is wealthy, it will eventually manifest wealth around you.

God is sending wealth harvesters, equipped with healthy, wealthy mindsets to break the shackles of poverty. These servants armed with a word from God will move with agility dominating world spheres that would otherwise be controlled by the world. However, you must fight! This was the most difficult chapter of this book to write. I petitioned God because I was sick of the warfare attached to it; it was so hard. In mid-complaint, I looked up to see a man breaking up soil with a plow across the street. I heard God say, "plow through." Plowing through is defined as "finishing something that takes a long time and is difficult." It means to move through something with a lot of difficulty.

I know it's hard but plow through. Lift your head, square your shoulders, stick out your chest, and go. Pick up your powerful weapons and infiltrate. You have everything you need to permeate the spheres of this world with the love of Jesus Christ. You have a wealth of knowledge living in your earthen vessel awaiting to come forth and feed a dying and impoverished world, the Truth.

12

KINGDOM PHILANTHROPISTS

I PASSIONATELY BELIEVE THAT the institution of tithing is an open invitation for the blessings of God to pour forth in our lives. While no longer a requirement today, sowing seed—ten percent—into good ground is a summons to the favor of the Lord (see 2 Corinthians 9). To be clear, blessings are not evoked because of any religious ritual but because of the selflessness and obedience giving embodies. We see an example of this free-will giving in the Book of Genesis. Abraham gave ten percent of his spoils from a battle to Melchizedek, the king of Justice (see Genesis 14:20). Melchizedek attempted to reject this offering, but Abraham insisted. Abraham didn't view his benevolence as only a gift to a human being. He considered his giving an act of worship to his God for all He had done for him. His giving wasn't prompted by sensationalism or manipulation but from his heart and according to his increase.

> *Let each one give [thoughtfully and with purpose] just as he has decided in his heart, not grudgingly or under compulsion, for God loves a cheerful giver [and delights in the one whose heart is in his gift].*

> *2 Corinthians 9:7*

Years ago, I sat in numerous church audiences with my best seed in hand only to be made to feel as it wasn't good enough. And other times I sowed, went home, and waited on the "blessing" I was told I'd receive as a result of sowing into the word that went forth. I saw no such harvest. There are bleeding people sitting in congregations worldwide waiting on a magical genie to fulfill their needs because they placed an offering into a tray. God is not a magical genie in a bottle. We cannot rub His belly and make three wishes. The truth is, while sowing is commendable in the eyes of the Lord, blessings can't be bought. Favor can't be franchised. Harvest time can't be hastened at the word of humans with ulterior motives. Only you and God are at liberty to decide what your "best" is. This is not up for debate with human beings. You are Spirit-led. You have an inner compass leading you in the right direction in all things. Scripture from both the Old and New Testament reveals that believers are to give according to their wealth.

> ♦ *All must give as they are able, according to the blessings given to them by the Lord your God.*

> *Deuteronomy 16:17*

♦ *So, the believers in Antioch decided to send relief to the brothers and sisters in Judea, everyone giving as much as they could.*

Acts 11:29

♦ *Whatever you give is acceptable if you give it eagerly. And give according to what you have, not what you don't have.*

2 Corinthians 8:12

It is also important to note that we must give to God in the right spirit. You can give millions grudgingly in your heart and reap absolutely nothing. You could sow two pennies and reap a harvest. Giving with a gracious, cheerful heart attracts the blessings and favor of the Lord.

Looking up, He saw the rich people putting their gifts into the treasury. And He saw a poor widow putting in two small copper coins. He said, "Truly I say to you, this poor widow has put in [proportionally] more than all of them. For they all put in gifts from their abundance; but she out of her poverty put in all she had to live on."

Luke 21:1-4

The Pharisees, hypocritical and vain were heavily influenced by the spirit of mammon. They were guilty of tossing coins into a tray so that those nearby would hear it. They placed a higher value on what man thought of them and less about what God already knew. Therefore, Scripture regards them as "covetous and lovers of money." The two mites given by the widow meant more to Jesus than the hundreds put in by the religious leaders. Why? The widow operated in selflessness and in all the religious leader's giving, they still operated in a spirit of poverty.

THE THREE TITHES

The Old Testament reveals that farmers were required to set aside a tenth of all the produce that was harvested yearly. The first Mosaic law on tithing is detailed below.

> *One-tenth of all crops belongs to the Lord, including the crops from fields and the fruit from trees. That one-tenth is holy to the Lord. If a person wants to get back [redeem] that tenth, one-fifth must be added to its price. The priest will take every [Every] tenth animal from a person's herd or flock, and it [a tenth of all that passes under the shepherd's rod,] will be holy to the Lord.*
>
> *Leviticus 27:30-32*

The first fruit of the crops could not be scattered at the discretion of the farmer. God designated specific places for the produce to be allocated. The Storehouse Tithe (Levitical Tithe) was to be presented to the Levites who ministered in the Temple of God (see Nehemiah 10:36). This tithe is given under the priesthood of Melchizedek because it's consecrated unto God for the continuance and maintenance of His house. The Storehouse Tithe serves as a facilitator of justice, setting captives free by funding Godly initiatives.

For the most part, the practice of tithing in the place of worship is often emphasized and adhered to. However, Scripture reveals that the Israelite's tithe did not end at ten percent. In fact, they sowed upwards to twenty-five percent of their harvest. There are three distinct tithes mentioned in

Scripture. The second tithe is mentioned in Leviticus 14:22-23. It reads:

> *Be sure to save [set aside/apart] one-tenth [a tithe] of all your crops [the produce/yield of your seed of the field] each year. Eat it in the presence of the Lord your God in the place where he chooses to be worshiped [cause his name to dwell; Zion]. Eat the tenth [tithe] of your grain, new wine, and oil, and eat the animals born first to your herds and flocks.*

The Pilgrimage Tithe (Festival Tithe) was set aside for the annual holy festivals ordained by God. Its purpose was to fund the enhancement of their relationships with God. The festivals were a time of celebration and experiencing enjoyment in the Lord. The cost of these festivals could be relatively expensive, so the tithe was saved to be used for food and lodging. Today for us, this tithe could be attributed as funds set aside for the yearly attendance of Christian conferences, retreats, events, and social gatherings.

Aside from the storehouse and pilgrimage tithe, there is a third tithe mentioned in Deuteronomy 26:12.

> *Bring [finish paying] a tenth [tithe] of all your harvest the third year (the year to give a tenth [tithe] of your harvest). Give it to the Levites, foreigners [resident aliens], orphans, and widows so that they may eat in your towns [gates] and be full.*

The Poor Tithe was to be used to feed and support the underprivileged (see also Deuteronomy 14:28-29). For the sake of the poor in the land, produce was placed in a storeroom for administration every three years. This suggests that a portion of our wealth should not only be sown to the leaders in the house of God. It should not only be laid aside for the enhancement of our relationship with Him, but we are also called to sow in the lives of those around us gripped by the shackles of poverty. Malachi 3:10-11 commands:

> *Bring all the tithes (the tenth) into the storehouse, so that there may be food in My house, and test Me in this," says the Lord of hosts, "if I will not open for you the windows of heaven for you [so great] a blessing until there is no more room to receive it. Then I will rebuke the devourer (insects, plague) for your sake and he will not destroy the fruits of the ground, nor will your vine in the field drop its grapes [before harvest]," says the Lord of hosts.*

The Hebrew word for "house" as used above is [16]*bayith.* *Bayith* applies to a house but in a wide variety of applications. I found interesting that bayith not only included the high places of "palaces," but also expanded to the "courts, tombs, dungeons, and prisons." This suggests that the storehouse of God is not limited to church buildings constructed by human hands. The storehouse not only includes the high places and palaces but reaches down to the low places. It extends to the tombs cursing poverty. It reaches the dungeons breaking the shackles of destitution. It goes into prison cells setting lives free from the bondage of lack. It even reaches into the courtrooms and executes justice defending the poor and the needy. However, sadly many limit the storehouse to the four walls of the church and even worse, the four walls of their homes.

> *Israel's watchmen are blind, they are all without knowledge. They are all mute dogs, they cannot bark; Panting, lying down, they love to slumber. And the dogs are greedy; they [never have enough. They are shepherds who have no*

understanding. They have all turned to their own way, each one to his unlawful gain without exception.

Isaiah 56:10-12

Scripture reveals many instances where the rich and the powerful of the land cheated the poor. Likewise, many have become self-serving, selfish individuals only concerned with filling their own bellies. A great injustice has taken place amongst the people of God. More than I'd like to mention, I've seen the poor exploited and the flock of God fleeced. But the King of Justice has heard the cry of His people. He has heard their stomachs growling; He has seen their tears falling. He has seen their hearts bleeding. He has heard their blood crying out to Him from the ground spilled by the hand of the very people called to protect them.

Defend the poor and fatherless: do justice to the afflicted and needy.

Psalm 82:3, KJV

The Hebrew word for charity is *tzedakah* and comes from the root word *tz-d-k* which means "justice." Justice and charity are synonymous. God has raised up wealth harvesters who will be used as instruments of justice in the earth. As in the days of Solomon when he operated in God-given wisdom to judge between right and wrong, so will you. You will see the needs that many choose to ignore; you will have the capacity, compassion, and innovativeness required to do something about it.

In the Book of Luke Jesus tells a parable of a wicked manager whose job, like Joseph, was an administrator/CEO of the household. The word "administration," is the Greek word

[17]*oikonomia* which means "economy" or "dispensation." Dispensation is defined as "something that is distributed or given out, a certain order, system, or arrangement." The manager was to act as a wealth dispenser; his job was to harvest wealth. However, instead of harvesting his supervisor's wealth, he squandered it. Because of his negligence, the manager feared the loss of his employment. He devised a shrewd scheme to cover his tracks in the event he found himself jobless. Surprisingly, the supervisor was pleased with his devious methods. Luke 16: 8-9 says:

> *And the lord commended the unjust steward, because he had done wisely: for the children of this world are in their generation wiser than the children of light. I tell you, use worldly wealth to gain friends for yourselves, so that when it is gone, you will be welcomed into eternal dwellings.*

At first glance, it would appear as though Jesus is instructing His disciples to become friends with the world with unrighteous money. However, the word "friends" as used here is from the Greek word *philos*, which means love. So, Jesus is saying that while there are those who mishandle wealth for their own personal misdeeds, we are to love people and use worldly wealth for eternal purposes. The Amplified version says, "use material resources as a way to further the work of God." God's managers, wealth harvesters, have a heavenly mandate to use the treasure in us to produce the prize of eternal treasure around us. With wealth, we can "make friends" with the goal of drawing them into conversion. Simply put, the wealth we use on earth has the potential to draw the wealth of souls into heaven for all of eternity.

THE GIFT OF GIVING

...Whoever has the gift of giving to others should give freely [generously].

Romans 12:8b

God is calling us away from benefiting from each other by the recycling of tithes and offerings. There is something more that He is requiring in this season. Just as God raises up pastors, prophets, apostles, teachers, and evangelists, He raises those with the gift of giving. These special givers give beyond the realm of tithes and offerings. Where tithes end, the harvester's wealth extends. And in this hour God is increasing them with wealth to operate as kingdom philanthropists.

The term "philanthropy" comes from two Greek roots, *Philos* and *Anthropos*. Again, Philos means "love," and Anthropos translates as "humankind." So, philanthropy is established in the love for humankind. Philanthropists extend aid to humanity, which is not based upon race, creed, religion, or nationality.

> *And if I have the gift of prophecy [and speak a new message from God to the people], and understand all mysteries, and [possess] all knowledge; and if I have all [sufficient] faith so that I can remove mountains, but do not have love [reaching out to others], I am nothing.*

1 Corinthians 13:2

What distinguishes kingdom philanthropists from others who give extravagantly is the posture of the heart. In fact, a genuine test that proves whether you are truly called a wealth harvester is the test of the heart. Kingdom philanthropy is rooted and grounded in real love, not emotionalism. Those called to this dispensation will have tremendous hearts of giving to match. They don't give out of necessity; they give with magnificent pleasure. Wealth is used as an instrument of righteousness. Our desire is to see God's kingdom expanded, not our own. Our goal is to make His name great, not our own. Our purpose is that His will is accomplished, not our own. As kingdom philanthropists, His love must always be the motivation behind our charitable endeavors. Impure agendas will result in weeds and thorns in the land of your harvest. Hebrews 6:7-8 says:

> *For men's hearts are just like the soil that drinks up the showers which often fall upon it. Some soil will yield crops as God's blessing upon the field. But if the field continues to produce only thorns and thistles a curse hangs over it and it will be burned.*

Philanthropy not only involves love for humankind, but it also involves "advancement," which are *"manifested"* by donations of money, property or work to needy persons." The charity of a kingdom philanthropist is motivated by the addition of lives in the kingdom of God. Love is an action word; love is not only what it says, but what it does. Love causes us to feel compassion, but the heart of the kingdom philanthropist moves beyond feelings. Kingdom philanthropists step beyond the place of *only* offering prayer when there are evident needs that can readily be met by our wallets. James 2:15-16 says it best:

> *Suppose there are brothers or sisters who need clothes and don't have enough to eat. What good is there in your saying to them "God bless you! Keep warm and eat well- if you don't give the necessities of life?*

Kingdom philanthropists are experts at closing their mouths and opening their wallets. They don't look out for their own interests but for the interests of others (see 1 Corinthians 10:24).

Many are familiar with the story of Ruth and Boaz. We know that Ruth, a Moabitess, came to the land of her mother-in-law, Naomi. Stricken with poverty, she was employed by Boaz—a wealthy landowner, and overseer. Her job was in the fields gleaning leftover sheaves left by the harvesters of his fields (see Ruth 2:5). One day while working, Ruth was noticed by Boaz and shown favor above the other gleaners. Ruth 2:16 says:

> *Also, you shall purposely pull out for her some stalks [of grain] from the sheaves and leave them so that she may collect them, and do not rebuke her.*

One version says that Boaz ordered his harvesters to leave "handfuls on purpose," for Ruth to glean. This was no new practice. Leviticus 19:9-10 says:

> *Now when you reap the harvest of your land, you shall not reap to the very corners of your field, nor shall you gather the gleanings (grain left after reaping) of your harvest. And you shall not glean your vineyard, nor shall you gather its fallen grapes; you shall leave them for the poor and for the stranger. I am the Lord your God.*

Jesus, the Lord of the Harvest, requires the harvesters He oversees to leave handfuls on purpose for the needy of this earth. Because "the righteous man cares for the rights of the poor, but the wicked man has no interest in such knowledge (Proverbs 29:7). If you have been in the fire, the wind, the darkness and the deep, you qualify to execute justice with the weapon of wealth. The deep has enlarged the capacity of your heart to hold and distribute wealth; you are a wealth dispenser. The wind has blown away your resistance. The waves have crashed your motives; they've drowned. The fire has blazed your feet; you have golden oil for your golden assignment. Now you're able to sympathize with those in need. When they hurt, you hurt. You've felt the weight of lack; you have the heart to destroy it.

KINGDOM PHILANTHROPIST EMERGE!

Kingdom-minded philanthropists are emerging to fill in the gap between lost souls and kingdom obligations. They are ascending not only with powerful prayers and prophetic words in their mouths but with wealth in their hands. They are coming forth with truth and in justice. Philanthropists are arising with the compassion of the Father in their hearts. They are arising to raise principles of giving and to add a wealth of souls to the kingdom of God. Foundations, businesses, Fortune 500 companies, para-church ministries, and television networks are surfacing. Best-selling authors are arising, inventions are being conceived in our hearts, multi-million-dollar visions are being drafted, blueprints are being laid out. Whatever good land God chose for you is before you. Goodness will be birthed in and through you. And because God loves a cheerful giver, your well will never run dry. Increase is your portion. 2 Corinthians 9:8b-11 (EXB) promises:

> *Then you will always have plenty of everything [in all things at all times you will*

have all you need]—enough to give to [abounding/overflowing in] every good work. [For] God is the One who gives seed to the farmer and bread for food. He will give you all the seed you need and make it grow [supply and multiply your seed]so there will be a great harvest from your goodness [of your righteousness]. He will make you rich in every way so that you can always give freely [generously].

Those attached to your life will be released into the knowledge of Jesus Christ as a result of your generosity. For as long as you sow, God will provide seed. And wherever there is kingdom seed, there will always be a kingdom harvest.

AFTERWORD

I T IS MY PRAYER that this book has served as confirmation in your heart. I pray that the harvester in you has been awakened and that you are ready and equipped to shift kingdoms for the glory of God. As you apply the principles of the Word of God in your life, I pray that He blesses you abundantly. I ask that He shines the light of His glory upon your countenance. May the manifold wisdom of the Lord flood your being so that you, in turn, flood His kingdom with wealth and resources unheard of. And as the Lord prepares you to emerge, I encourage you to stay in the Potter's hands so that you can bless those who are being buried in potter's field.

In His Love,

Alisha N. Scott

Notes

INTRODUCTION

[1] Emerge: https://www.dictionary.com/browse/emerge

[2] Harvesting: https://en.wikipedia.org/wiki/Harvest

[3] Purge: https://www.dictionary.com/browse/purge

[4] Reaping: https://en.m.wikipedia.org/wiki/Harvest

CHAPTER 1: BEAUTIFUL RUINS

[5] Trade Wind History: https://en.m.wikipedia.org/wiki/Trade wind

[6] Willie Wonka: https://en.wikipedia.org/wiki/the_Chocolate_Factory

[7] Goad: https://en.wikipedia.org/wiki/Goad

CHAPTER 2: WEALTHY RUINS

[8] Ocean's Floor Wealth:www.forbes.com/sites/trevornace/2017/09/15/771-trillion-worth-gold-hidden-ocean/amp/

[9] Deep: https://www.dictionary.com/browse/deep

[10] Mayim: Strong's Hebrew Lexicon (KJV) H432

CHAPTER 3: DEATH VALLEY

[11] Death Valley Furnace Creek: https://en.m.wikipedia.org/wiki/furnace

[12] Midbar: Strong's 4057, place of order, to speak

CHAPTER 4: THE HARVESTING BLUEPRINT

[13] Polupoikilos: https://biblehub.com/greek/4182.htm

CHAPTER 6: KINGLY PITFALLS

[14] Aven: https://www.biblestudytools.com/dictionary/aven/

CHAPTER 8: VESSEL OF WEALTH

[15] Potter's Wheel: https://en.m.wikipedia.org/wiki/Potter's_wheel

CHAPTER 12: KINGDOM PHILANTHROPISTS

[16] Bayith: https://www.biblestudytools.com/lexicons/hebrew/nas/bayith

[17] Oikonomia: https://www.aeaweb.org/articles?id=10.1257/jep.30.1